THE LOW-CARB
CookwoRx Cookbook

ALSO BY THE EADES

THE LOW-CARB
CookwoR_X Cookbook

Mary Dan Eades, M.D.
and
Michael R. Eades, M.D.

WILEY

John Wiley & Sons, Inc.

Published by John Wiley & Sons, Inc., Hoboken, New Jersey
Published simultaneously in Canada

Design and composition by Navta Associates, Inc.

Roasted Red Pepper Soup on page 82 is adapted from Chilled Red Pepper Soup with Cilantro in *Protein Power* published by Bantam Books in 1996.

For general information about our other products and services, please contact our Customer Care Department within the United States at (800) 762-2974, outside the United States at (317) 572-3993 or fax (317) 572-4002.

Wiley also publishes its books in a variety of electronic formats. Some content that appears in print may not be available in electronic books. For more information about Wiley products, visit our web site at www.wiley.com.

Library of Congress Cataloging-in-Publication Data:

Eades, Mary Dan.
    The low-carb cookworRx cookbook / Mary Dan Eades and Michael R. Eades.
        p. cm.
    Includes index.
    ISBN-13 978-0-471-74074-2 (cloth)
    ISBN-10 0-471-74074-8 (cloth)
1. Cookery. 2. Low-carbohydrate diet—Recipes. I. Eades, Michael R. II. Title.
    TX714.E216 2005
    641.5' 6383—dc22   2005021553

Printed in the United States of America

10 9 8 7 6 5 4 3 2 1

Dedicated to our daughters-in-law,

Jamye and Katherine.

We're glad you chose to join our pack.

Contents

Acknowledgments

It takes a village to produce a book, and we wish to gratefully acknowledge that fact. To our tireless agents, Channa Taub and Carol Mann, our thanks for another job well done. To Tom Miller, our editor, and all the copy editors, graphic artists, designers, and sales and marketing people at John Wiley & Sons who worked under tight deadlines to help us hone and shape this book and get it to market on time, we appreciate all your help and good work.

This book is, of course, the companion cookbook to our PBS television series. And if it takes a village to make a book, it takes a whole city to produce a television show. We'd like to acknowledge some of the many people who made the CookwoRx television series possible. First and foremost, to those who believed enough in the concept to help us make it a show in the first place: our production partners, cocreators, and friends Gregg Shelby and Michael Radocha, Jr., and the good folks at Milwaukee Public Television—Ellis Bromberg, general manager; Tom Dvorak, director of programming; Raul Galvan, manager of program production; and Dan Dvorak, manager of production. Without them we wouldn't have a cooking and nutrition show. Their unending willingness to go the extra mile made the difference. However, without the group that follows, none of it would have ever happened. Our thanks and appreciation for cheerful excellence go to: Kathy Hannemann, stylist; Gary Schrubbe, executive chef; Steve Farout, sous chef; Enrique Heard, assistant to the chefs; Scott Buss, production coordinator;

Heike Heemann-Radocha, Jane Beck, and Timm Gable, production assistants; Glenn P. Riley, lighting and remote supervisor; Tony Banks, floor director; Melvin Verhein, Diane R. Martin, and Duane J. Rodriguez on the cameras; Brian R. McArthur, senior production engineer; Jerry Meilke, audio production engineer; Al Zoril, videotape engineer; Greg Haladej, vision mixer; Thay Yang, graphics; Linda Murphy and Jeff Moorbeck, editors; and the countless other people whose names we might not have known but who helped to move the show along. Thanks to you all.

And, as always, thanks to our faithful assistant, Kristi McAfee, who handles all the million details of our life and business, ever with a smile.

Last, but never least, thanks to our sons, daughters-in-law, and the grandangels for giving us the real reason we keep on keepin' on.

◇   ◇   ◇

Introduction

The best thing you can do for your health is to spend more time in your own kitchen. That's the sentiment we believe will serve as the cornerstone principle for solving the nation's rapidly escalating obesity and related health crises. With twenty years of clinical expertise in teaching low-carb nutrition to our patients, we've long known *what* to tell them to eat. Now, drawing on twenty years of culinary experience in our own low-carb kitchen, we're ready to teach them *how*. It's always been our fervent belief that the road to success on a low-carb diet—or any diet for that matter—goes straight through the kitchen. The reasons for that belief are several, but chief among them is the inescapable fact that if you make your own food, you know what's in it. A home-cooked meal allows you to fully control both its quality and quantity, reducing or eliminating the chance of your progress being undermined by hidden sugars or starches, unacceptable sweeteners, powdered egg yolks, unhealthy trans fats, and other assorted preserving, stabilizing, and flavor-enhancing ingredients commonly found in mass-produced factory food.

Perhaps more importantly, however, learning to cook tasty low-carb meals will foster greater long-term success in maintaining the weight loss and improved health that drew you to the diet in the first place. No matter how powerful a tool a low-carb diet may be to control weight and restore health in the short run—and there's absolutely no doubt that it is the easiest and fastest way to achieve those goals—the regimen won't stick as a lifestyle change until it becomes not just a way to eat for the six weeks or six months necessary to achieve some specific health or weight goal, but the way you eat, live, and cook in your own kitchen day in and day out from now on.

The new techniques you'll need to begin cooking healthy low-carb meals are simple and easy to master. We designed them that way because we wanted them to be useful to everyone, and because we are not trained chefs; we're just committed low-carb dieters who love to eat, love to cook, and enjoy being together in the kitchen. (Okay, we're experts in the medical and nutritional aspects of low-carb dieting, too, but that doesn't help you much when the muffins are burning.) Cooking the low-carb way doesn't require that you abandon wholesale all that you know about cooking, just that you expand your knowledge base by learning a few new techniques, especially with regard to making baked goods, sweets, and breakfast treats. Chief among these is the trick of replacing some or all of the highest-carb staples—for example, sugars, flour, and other cereal grains—with foods of better nutritional quality and fewer carb grams in ways that preserve the integrity, taste, texture, and mouthfeel of the original version. You'll find many of the tips we've learned about making these substitutions and the whys and wherefores of low-carb cooking in the introductory text to the individual chapters that relate most closely to those foods. There, too, you'll find many of the little nutritional facts that will help to bolster your resolve to eat well.

As we've adapted most traditionally high-carb recipes into low- (or at least lower-) carb versions, our goal has been to reduce the carb load per serving by 50 percent to 75 percent or more and to retain the quality of the dish in a reasonable quantity. To us, there's no value in creating an ultra-low-carb recipe with all the taste and appeal of a cardboard box or playground sand. Nor is there any benefit in dividing a normal-size portion of something into fifteen crumbs that we can disingenuously call "low carb." We'd simply rather take a pass on that kind of food; there are too many delicious, naturally low-carb foods out there to enjoy. Our guiding principle in developing low-carb recipes is and will remain to make them as good or almost as good as the original and significantly lower in carb.

Clearly, there's a bit of a learning curve to be negotiated in making such adaptations—turning out a tasty scone with a good crumb with one-fourth the flour can't be accomplished without a little trial and error, after all. But fear not, we've done the heavy lifting for you and created dozens of easy-to-use recipes for a full array of delicious low-carb imposters that (to borrow a line from a pasta sauce ad) will let you bring something wonderful to your table again—your family.

It all comes back to the guiding philosophy that led us to launch our *Low Carb CookwoRx* television show in the first place and that you'll find echoed throughout this book: the best thing you can do for your health is to spend more time in your own kitchen because if you make the meal yourself, you know what's in it, and it's really the only way to know what's in it.

CHAPTER 1

◇ ◇ ◇

Bread, Muffins, and More

◇ ◇ ◇

◇   ◇   ◇

The traditional low-carb diet—at least as we've always prescribed it—is a rich and varied one, completely satisfying in every respect except one: the absence of bread. In times past, while dieters certainly bemoaned the lack, once committed to the plan, they resolved to hold the toast at breakfast and pretty much accepted that they could no longer tear into a crusty roll at dinner or drop by the neighborhood coffee bar to enjoy a muffin or a scone with a cup of java. For some, probably for most, the sacrifice, while difficult, was worth the reward of a leaner, healthier body and the pleasure of feeling good again; for others, abandoning bread and baked goods proved an insurmountable obstacle to their success on a low-carb plan. Fortunately all that has changed.

Although better products are now coming to the market, that wasn't always the case; until very recently, the commercial low-carb breads and baked goods available were practically inedible. We'd rather have done without for all eternity than eaten them, and admittedly, many still fall into that category. And to top it off, there weren't even any reliable recipe techniques known for making low-carb bread products at home. We recall some really awful pseudobread recipes based on meringue that we never could get to turn out no matter how hard we tried. But practice makes perfect, and we've learned a thing or two in the last twenty-odd years, much of it from our previous collaboration with Ursula Solom on the *Low-Carb Comfort Food Cookbook*. Inspired by some of her ingenious techniques and drawing upon the suggestions of other friends and colleagues, we dove into baking in a big way in recent years. What we discovered is that low-carb baking is not as big a challenge as we'd thought. Once you get a handle on the general idea, it's easier than you might imagine to transform most of your favorite higher-carb baked goods into lower-carb ones.

First and foremost, making good reduced-carb baked goods demands learning how to make some substitutions, particularly for the wheat flour that forms the bulk of breads, coffee cakes, muffins, scones, waffles, and pancakes. Our go-to alternative, as you'll see in these recipes, is almond flour, which is nothing more than finely ground blanched (or not) almonds—very healthy, nutritious, and low in carb. You can find almond flour or meal in most grocery or natural food stores nowadays; usually it's in the baking aisle alongside the various other kinds of meals and flours. If it's not there, ask your grocer to order it or go online, where you'll find dozens of sources from which you can order it by mail.

Denser and higher in protein, fat, and fiber (and calories) than wheat flour, almond flour works perfectly to add heft and bulk to almost any sort of batter or dough. We use it to replace half to two-thirds of the flour in most of our baked goods recipes. Granted, it doesn't have all the same properties as the flours made from grains; cakes made with it won't be as light and airy, for instance, and may need a bit more leavening agent in order to poof properly. Almond meal's oilier nature also makes it somewhat water repellent instead of water attractive like starches and sugars. Almond flour does have certain advantages, however. Because it has a naturally higher fat content, it allows us to reduce the amount of added butter or oil in most recipes, which in a small way helps to offset some of the cost difference between almond flour and wheat flour. Good health is more expensive, but, to paraphrase an ad, you're darn well worth it.

Along with the almond meal, our baked goods recipes call for mixing in one or more low-carb impostor ingredients. We might use low-carb whey protein powder, vital wheat gluten, oat bran, rice bran; certain thickening, bulking, and water-attracting agents such as xanthan gum, guar gum, polydextrose, and ThickenThin products; or even a bit of the real thing (that is, wheat flour) to create a dry ingredient mixture with the flourlike qualities that give us the right taste, feel, and look of the original with substantially fewer effective (net) carb grams. Our rule of thumb in adapting or developing new recipes for baked goods is to begin by replacing half the flour called for with almond meal and then replacing the other half with varying combinations of the impostor ingredients.

All of the impostors are readily available at the grocery store, with the possible exception of the fiber thickeners. Many grocery and most natural food stores will carry xanthan gum and guar gum; you can check low-carb specialty stores or go online to find polydextrose or the ThickenThin products mentioned in many of the recipes. You should be able to readily find all the ingredients, but if you come up dry, check our Web sites, www.lowcarbcookworx.com and www.proteinpower.com. An alternative to ThickenThin not/Sugar is 2 tablespoons of a mixture of equal parts of xanthan gum, guar gum, and powdered egg whites. It won't be exactly the same, but it will work pretty well in most, but not all, recipes.

Just about any bakery recipe can be low-carb adapted with these kinds of substitutions. One possible exception might be puff pastry; so far we haven't attempted an adaptation. After you've followed these recipes a time or two, you will pick up on the similarities between them and the general techniques of replacing flour in recipes. While it does sometimes take a little bit of tweaking of imposter amounts and a few attempts to get an adapted recipe to work for you, keep at it. Before you know it, you'll be turning out a lower-carb version of your favorite aunt's banana nut bread or the cherry nut muffins you once enjoyed (in your pre-low-carb days) at the corner coffee shop. When you do, share your knowledge with others: we invite you to post your recipes on our Web site, www.proteinpower.com. If it's a really great recipe, we just might use it on the show . . . with proper credit given, of course!

Most of the recipes you'll find in this chapter will freeze well and can be reheated quickly, which is a great benefit for busy people accustomed to grabbing a bagel or a muffin on the way to work.

Actually, we think our muffins, waffles, and coffee cakes are better than the real thing because they're more protein rich and satisfying than the higher-carb originals they replace. Two Cinnamon-Piñon Power Muffins, for instance, provide 26 grams of protein and only 14 grams of effective carbohydrate; that's a full meal's worth—enough to fill you up and satisfy your appetite quite nicely.

We're sure that the recipes you'll find here will help you to make good nutrition convenient once again.

Almond Drop Scones

MAKES 1 DOZEN
SCONES
SERVES 6
(2 SCONES EACH)

These quick and easy gems are not only delicious but also full enough of protein and good fats that a couple of them, with a cup of steaming coffee, make a quick and healthy breakfast or afternoon snack. Make several batches at once, as they'll freeze well.

Protein per serving:
12 grams

Effective carb per serving:
6 grams

¼ cup almond flour
¼ cup flax meal
¼ cup whole-wheat or rice flour
¼ cup whey protein powder
½ teaspoon baking powder
1 tablespoon granular Splenda
⅜ teaspoon salt
1 tablespoon ThickenThin not/Sugar (see page 9) or 1 teaspoon xanthan gum
3 tablespoons cold unsalted butter, cut into small chunks
1 egg
⅓ cup half-and-half

Preheat the oven to 400 degrees.

Mix all the dry ingredients together in a bowl.

Cut in the cold butter chunks until the dry mixture resembles coarse meal (your fingers work well for this).

In a separate small bowl, beat the egg and combine it with the half-and-half. Pour the egg–half-and-half mixture into the dry ingredients.

Mix with a fork until just combined.

Drop by heaping tablespoons onto a buttered or parchment-lined baking sheet.

Bake for 12 to 15 minutes until lightly browned.

Serve warm with butter or allow to cool completely and freeze, separated on a baking tray. Then store the scones in the freezer in an airtight container for single serving ease. Thaw them in the refrigerator overnight and gently rewarm in the oven or the microwave.

Classic Currant-Walnut Scones

MAKES 1 DOZEN
SCONES

So dense, crumbly, and rich you'll never suspect these scones are low in carb. We love to eat them warm alongside a good cup of steaming espresso or Americano for an afternoon pick-me-up snack, but they're great for breakfast, too.

Protein per serving:
10.3 grams

Effective carb per serving:
10.3 grams

2 cups almond flour
½ cup whole-wheat flour
1 tablespoon baking powder
6 packets Splenda
¼ teaspoon salt
⅓ cup finely chopped walnuts
¼ cup dried currants
10 tablespoons unsalted butter, cold
½ cup heavy cream
3 large egg yolks
1 teaspoon pure vanilla extract

Preheat the oven to 425 degrees.

Combine all the dry ingredients, except the nuts and currants, in a large mixing bowl.

Cut the butter into small cubes.

Working quickly, cut the butter into the dry mixture with a fork or your fingertips until it reaches the consistency of coarse meal (with a few butter pebbles remaining).

In a measuring cup, lightly beat the cream with the egg yolks and vanilla.

Make a well in the center of the dry ingredients in the bowl.

Pour the cream mixture into the well and with a fork, gently bring the dry ingredients into the wet mixture until just combined. Add the nuts and currants. Do not overmix or the scones will be tough.

Turn out onto a board dusted with a bit of almond flour and sprinkle a bit more almond flour on top of the wet dough.

Very gently, knead the dough by folding over and flattening it slightly just a couple of times. Again, do not overdo it or the cakes will be tough.

Gently flatten the dough into a circle about ¾ inch thick.

Cut three times across the diameter, as you would a pie, to make 6 triangles, then cut each triangle in half.

Place the scones on a parchment-lined or buttered baking sheet and bake for 20 to 25 minutes.

Serve warm with butter.

Basic Muffins

MAKES 1 DOZEN
MUFFINS

Plain and simple, this basic recipe makes the kind of muffins kids will love—no lumps, no chunks, no shocking colors they'll want to pick out. They won't know that the whey protein, eggs, and dairy products make them a filling breakfast or snack you'll feel good about feeding them. From this basic recipe, you can let your imagination take flight with additions to please a more sophisticated palate, young or old. Make a double batch; they freeze well in a ziplock freezer bag. Reheat them gently in the toaster oven or the microwave.

Protein per serving:
12 grams

Effective carb per serving:
6 grams

¼ cup whole-wheat flour

1½ cups almond flour

¼ cup whey protein powder

3 teaspoons baking powder

12 packets Splenda

1 tablespoon ThickenThin not/Sugar (see page 9) or 1 teaspoon xanthan gum

½ teaspoon salt

3 tablespoons unsalted butter, melted

2 eggs

2 ounces cream cheese

¼ cup half-and-half

¼ cup water

Preheat the oven to 400 degrees.

Grease a standard 12-cup muffin tin with coconut oil or butter. If you prefer, line the cups with paper baking cups.

Mix all the dry ingredients together in a bowl.

In a separate bowl, mix the melted butter, eggs, cream cheese, half-and-half, and water.

By hand, fold the dry ingredients into the wet ones, mixing until moist, but do not beat.

Pour the batter into the prepared cups of the muffin tin, filling them ⅔ to ¾ full.

Bake for 20 to 25 minutes until golden brown. A toothpick inserted into the center should come out clean.

Cranberry-Orange Power Muffins

MAKES 1 DOZEN
MUFFINS

The tang of cranberry and the refreshing scent of orange zest make these muffins especially appealing in the fall and the winter, but don't be surprised if you find yourself making batches of them in every season. They are delicious, filling, and quick.

Protein per serving:
10.1 grams

Effective carb per serving:
7 grams

¼ cup whole-wheat flour
1½ cups almond flour
¼ cup whey protein powder
3 teaspoons baking powder
⅛ teaspoon freshly grated nutmeg
16 packets Splenda
1 tablespoon ThickenThin not/Sugar (see page 9) or 1 teaspoon
   xanthan gum
½ teaspoon salt
2 ounces cream cheese, softened
2 eggs
3 tablespoons unsalted butter, melted
¼ cup half-and-half
1 orange, zest only
¼ cup water
1 cup fresh or frozen cranberries, coarsely chopped

Preheat the oven to 400 degrees.

Grease a standard 12-cup muffin tin with coconut oil or butter. If you prefer, line the cups with paper baking cups.

Mix all the dry ingredients together in a bowl.

In a separate bowl, beat the cream cheese until smooth. Add the eggs and then the melted butter, beating until smooth; finally, beat in the half-and-half, orange zest, and water.

By hand, fold the dry ingredients into the wet ones, mixing until just moist, but do not beat.

Gently fold in the cranberries.

Pour the batter into the prepared cups of the muffin tin, filling them ⅔ to ¾ full.

Bake for 20 to 25 minutes until golden brown. A toothpick inserted into the center should come out clean.

Lemon-Blueberry Power Muffins

MAKES 1 DOZEN
MUFFINS

These tart and fruity muffins have all the taste of the original but pack enough protein that two will make a meal. Make several batches because they freeze well, and, if your house is anything like ours, they'll go fast.

Protein per serving:
12 grams

Effective grams per serving:
7.9 grams

¼ cup whole-wheat flour

1½ cups almond flour

¼ cup whey protein powder

3 teaspoons baking powder

16 packets Splenda

1 tablespoon ThickenThin not/Sugar (see page 9) or 1 teaspoon xanthan gum

½ teaspoon salt

2 ounces cream cheese, softened

2 eggs

3 tablespoons unsalted butter, melted

¼ cup half-and-half

1 lemon, juice and zest

1 cup fresh or frozen blueberries

Preheat the oven to 400 degrees.

Grease a standard 12-cup muffin tin with coconut oil or butter. If you prefer, line the cups with paper baking cups instead.

Mix all the dry ingredients together in a bowl.

In a separate bowl, beat the cream cheese until smooth. Add the eggs and then the melted butter, beating until smooth; finally, beat in the half-and-half, lemon juice, and lemon zest.

By hand, fold the dry ingredients into the wet ones, mixing until just moist, but do not beat.

Gently fold in the blueberries.

Pour the batter into the prepared cups of the muffin tin, filling them ⅔ to ¾ full.

Bake for 20 to 25 minutes until golden brown. A toothpick inserted into the center should come out clean.

Cinnamon-Piñon Power Muffins

MAKES 1 DOZEN
MUFFINS

These muffins have just a hint of the flavors of the biscochitos *(Spanish cookies) that have been served each Christmas for hundreds of years at the Palace of the Governors at the culmination of the Las Posadas de Santa Fe celebration. Rich in protein and controlled in carb, two of these muffins will make a fine meal on the run.*

Protein per serving:
13.1 grams

Effective carb per serving:
6.9 grams

½ cup piñon nuts
¼ cup whole-wheat flour
1½ cups almond flour
¼ cup whey protein powder
3 teaspoons baking powder
2 teaspoons cinnamon
⅛ teaspoon cayenne pepper
12 packets Splenda
1 tablespoon ThickenThin not/Sugar (see page 9) or 1 teaspoon xanthan gum
½ teaspoon salt
2 ounces cream cheese, softened
2 eggs
3 tablespoons unsalted butter, melted
¼ cup half-and-half
¼ cup water

Preheat the oven to 400 degrees.

Grease a standard 12-cup muffin tin with coconut oil or butter. If you prefer, line the cups with paper baking cups instead.

In a hot skillet, lightly toast the piñon nuts, shaking or stirring as needed, until just beginning to color. Keep a watchful eye, as they burn easily. Set aside to cool.

Mix all the dry ingredients, except the nuts, together in a bowl.

In a separate bowl, beat the cream cheese until smooth. Add the eggs and then the melted butter, beating until smooth; finally, beat in the half-and-half and water.

By hand, fold the dry ingredients into the wet ones, mixing until just moist, but do not beat.

Gently fold in the toasted nuts.

Pour the batter into the prepared cups of the muffin tin, filling them ⅔ to ¾ full.

Bake for 20 to 25 minutes until golden brown. A toothpick inserted into the center should come out clean.

Pecan-Cinnamon Coffee Cake

SERVES 12

This cake is perfect for a midafternoon snack with a cup of coffee or tea, and is hearty enough in protein that a slice can make a fast and filling breakfast on the run. Beware—at 300 calories a slice, this is not a low-calorie cake, but if you love coffee cake, this easy, quick recipe is sure to become one of your favorites. We enjoy it unglazed, but if a bit of extra sweetness melts your butter, top it with a drizzle of Bit O' Sweet Glaze (page 219).

Protein per serving:
11 grams

Effective carb per serving:
9.4 grams

STREUSEL
1 cup chopped pecans
1 tablespoon ThickenThin not/Sugar (see page 9)
¾ cup granular Splenda
1 teaspoon ground cinnamon
3 tablespoons unsalted butter, melted

BATTER
1 cup almond flour
¼ cup whole-wheat flour
¼ cup vital wheat gluten
¼ cup pecan meal
¼ cup low-carb whey protein powder, natural or vanilla flavor
1 tablespoon ThickenThin not/Sugar (see page 9) or 1 teaspoon xanthan gum
15 packets Splenda
1 teaspoon ground cinnamon
2 teaspoons baking powder
½ teaspoon salt
5 tablespoons unsalted butter, cut into small pieces
1 egg, well beaten
¾ cup half-and-half

Preheat the oven to 375 degrees.

Generously butter a 9-inch-square cake pan.

In a bowl, make the streusel by combining the chopped pecans and ThickenThin; stir to coat the nuts. Add the Splenda, 1 teaspoon of the cinnamon, and the melted butter; stir to combine and set aside.

In a separate bowl, combine all the dry ingredients for the batter.

Cut the butter into the dry batter ingredients with your fingertips or a fork until the mixture resembles coarse meal.

Add the egg to the butter-flour batter mixture and beat with an electric mixer on low speed. Add the half-and-half and continue beating just until blended.

Pour half of the batter into the buttered cake pan, top with one-half of the streusel mixture, then pour in the remaining batter, and finally the remaining streusel mixture.

Bake for about 30 minutes until a toothpick inserted into the center comes out clean.

Cool on a rack for at least 15 minutes before cutting.

Serve warm. The cake can be reheated, gently, in the microwave for 20 seconds.

Buckwheat Power Cakes

SERVES 4

Richer and heartier than ordinary pancakes and packed with good whey protein, a stack of these cakes will really make a meal. Top them with some melted butter, Almost-Real Maple Syrup (page 26), or Very Berry Syrup (page 28) for a filling breakfast, even without a side of bacon. In maintenance, you'll have enough carb room to spare for some berries or a mimosa cocktail.

Protein per serving:
27 grams

Effective carb per serving:
10 grams

⅓ cup buckwheat flour
⅓ cup almond flour
⅓ cup low-carb whey protein powder
3 packets Splenda
¼ teaspoon salt
1½ teaspoons baking powder
4 eggs, separated
⅜ cup water
⅜ cup half-and-half

Preheat a griddle or a large skillet over medium-low heat.

In a bowl, mix the dry ingredients together.

In a separate bowl, use an electric mixer to beat the egg whites until stiff. Set aside.

In another bowl, beat the yolks, water, and half-and-half together. Stir in the dry ingredients to blend. Gently fold in the egg whites, partially incorporating them but leaving some streaks of beaten egg white visible in the batter.

Melt a teaspoon or two of unsalted butter on the hot griddle, and when it foams, ladle on the batter by heaping tablespoonfuls, allowing room for the batter to spread slightly. Cook the power cakes until brown on the bottom, flip, and cook the other side until brown.

Serve immediately if possible; if necessary, hold in a warm (180- to 200-degree) oven for 10 to 15 minutes.

Almond-Pecan Waffles

MAKES ABOUT 6
SEVEN-INCH
WAFFLES

Quick and easy to stir up, these hearty waffles are so filled with protein and good fats that you'll hardly need a side of bacon or sausage. All by themselves, they make a filling breakfast that will get the day off to a good start. And because they freeze well, you can cook up a batch to freeze and have toaster waffles ready to go on those busy mornings. If you don't have time for syrup and a plate, try them with a smear of Hi-Pro Almond Yogurt Cream Spread (page 54) or commercial low-carb chocolate hazelnut spread for a breakfast on the run.

Protein per serving:
21.8 grams

Effective carb per serving:
6.2 grams (waffle only. Syrup, fruit, or other toppings will add extra carbs.)

1 cup almond flour
¼ cup finely chopped pecans
½ cup whey protein powder
1 teaspoon baking powder
4 ounces cream cheese
6 eggs
¼ cup heavy cream

Preheat a waffle iron, oiling if necessary to prevent sticking.

Mix the dry ingredients, including the nuts, together in a small bowl.

Beat the softened cream cheese and two eggs until smooth. Add the remaining eggs, one at a time, and beat thoroughly between additions.

Beat in the heavy cream.

Fold in the dry ingredients. Do not overbeat at this stage or the waffles will be tough.

Spoon about ⅓ cup of the batter into the hot waffle iron and cook for about 3 minutes until golden brown. These waffles will brown a little earlier than their high-carb cousins, so keep an eye on them.

Remove the waffles to a serving plate and top with Maple Surple (page 27), commercial low-carb syrup, or fresh fruit and whipped cream.

Lemon-Ricotta Flapjacks

SERVES 4

A dear friend of ours introduced us to the higher-carb original of this recipe and we fell in love. These delicate cakes are sweet, with a tart tang from the lemon zest. We enjoy them with homemade low-carb syrup or simply as they are with a bit of butter. Filled with protein and good fats, they're a satisfying meal even without bacon, sausage, or eggs.

Protein per serving:
30 grams

Effective carb per serving:
12.2 grams

1½ cups ricotta cheese
½ cup sour cream
3 eggs, separated
4 packets Splenda
1 large lemon, juice and zest
¼ teaspoon baking soda
¼ cup whole-wheat flour
½ cup almond flour
¼ cup whey protein powder
pinch salt (or to taste)

Preheat a griddle or a large skillet over medium-low heat.

In a large mixing bowl, beat the ricotta, sour cream, egg yolks, Splenda, lemon juice, and zest.

In a separate bowl, beat the egg whites until stiff peaks form.

In another bowl, combine all the dry ingredients.

By hand, stir the dry ingredients into the ricotta mixture, blending well. Do not beat.

Gently fold the egg whites into the batter, leaving some streaks of beaten egg white visible throughout.

Melt a teaspoon or two of butter on the hot griddle or skillet. When the butter foams slightly and is hot, ladle on the batter by heaping tablespoonfuls, allowing room for the batter to spread slightly.

Cook the flapjacks for 3 to 4 minutes until brown on the bottom and slightly dry on the top; flip and brown the other side.

Serve immediately with melted butter and low-carb syrup or a sprinkle of Splenda or stevia and some fresh berries.

Proatmeal

SERVES 2

In the cold of winter, there's nothing more satisfying in the morning than a big steaming bowl of hot cereal. Unfortunately for low carbers, especially those in the earliest and most restrictive phases of the diet, the gram counts exceed specified carb allowances. However, you can enjoy a delicious bowlful made with nut meals and whey that's as hearty and warming as the original and takes a far smaller bite from your carb budget. Although lower in carb, it's not low calorie, so enjoy in moderation.

Protein per serving:
40 grams

Effective carb per serving:
14 grams
(with raisins)

2 cups water
½ teaspoon salt
¾ cup walnut, almond, or pecan meal
¼ cup half-and-half
2 scoops (about 40 grams) natural or vanilla low-carb whey protein powder
2 tablespoons ThickenThin not/Cereal* (see page 9) or 2 teaspoons xanthan gum
2 packets Splenda (optional)
2 teaspoons unsalted butter
2 teaspoons sliced almonds, chopped walnuts, or pecans
2 teaspoons raisins (optional)

Bring the water to a rolling boil in a covered saucepan, then add the salt.

Slowly add the nut meal, stirring constantly to avoid forming lumps.

Reduce the heat to low and simmer, uncovered, for about 20 minutes until the mixture begins to reduce in volume and slightly thicken.

In a small bowl, mix the half-and-half with the whey protein powder and ThickenThin, stirring until smooth. Add the Splenda, if desired.

*ThickenThin not/Cereal is a fiber thickener that adds almost no usable carbohydrate to the finished product.

When the faux oats have cooked, add the butter and allow it to melt.

Remove from the heat and stir in the half-and-half mixture.

Divide the hot cereal equally between two bowls and top each with chopped nuts and raisins. Serve immediately.

Almost-Real Maple Syrup

SERVES 4

As the name suggests, this imposter is not quite as good as the pure Vermont original, but it's quite tasty nonetheless. It recalls the homemade burnt sugar syrup Momma used to make on Sunday morning . . . but without the metabolic mayhem promised by a cup of real sugar. And unlike its commercially produced low-carb cousins, it avoids the use of sugar alcohols and the gastrointestinal side effects they can cause.

Protein per serving:
0 grams

Effective carb per serving:
3 grams
(There is great debate about whether the carbs contained in the bulking agent —maltodextrin mainly—used in Splenda are absorbable as carb or not. We've counted them as if they are.)

2 cups water

1 cup granular Splenda

1 tablespoon ThickenThin not/Sugar (see page 9) or 1 teaspoon xanthan gum

1 tablespoon maple extract

In a medium saucepan, mix the water, Splenda, and ThickenThin and allow to thicken. (Adjust the amount of ThickenThin to achieve the desired syrup consistency.)

Add the maple extract and bring to a brief boil.

Reduce the heat to keep warm until ready to serve.

Maple Surple

SERVES 4

Roger Miller, one of our favorite entertainers, said it best: "Roses are red and violets are purple. Sugar's sweet and so's maple surple." We especially love to use this syrup on low-carb waffles, so the butter distributes evenly and doesn't get stuck in the holes.

Protein per serving:
0.2 gram

Effective carb per serving:
3.6 grams

2 cups Almost-Real Maple Syrup (page 26)
1 stick unsalted butter

In a medium saucepan, warm the syrup to a simmer.

Cut the butter into chunks, add to the warm syrup, and allow the butter to melt.

Stir to combine.

Serve immediately over pancakes, waffles, or French toast.

VARIATION

Substitute 2 teaspoons of almond extract for the maple extract and add ¼ cup of finely chopped pecans to make Almond Butter Pecan Surple.

Very Berry Syrup

SERVES 4

The perfect way to get kids to eat their fruit every day, this berry syrup is great over low-carb pancakes, waffles, or Hi-Pro French Toast Fingers (page 235). For kids of all ages, it's yummy over a dish of low-carb ice cream or stirred into yogurt. It's also a great way to flavor homemade yogurt "cream cheese."

Protein per serving:
0.6 gram

Effective carb per serving:
9.2 grams

1 package (10 ounces) frozen mixed berries, thawed
2 cups water (divided in half for use)
½ lemon, juice and zest
10 packets Splenda
1 tablespoon ThickenThin not/Sugar (see page 9) or 1 teaspoon
    xanthan gum

In a blender, combine the thawed berries, 1 cup of the water, and the lemon juice. Pulse until smooth.

Put the remaining cup of water into a saucepan over medium heat. Whisk in the Splenda and ThickenThin and allow the syrup to thicken. Add additional thickener by the teaspoonful if a thicker syrup is desired, bearing in mind that the fruit puree will add some thickness.

Add the pureed fruit and lemon zest.

Bring briefly to a boil, then reduce the heat to simmer until ready to serve.

CHAPTER 2

◇ ◇ ◇

Breakfast, Brunch, and Sometimes Lunch

Omelet Caprese

Farmer's Veggie Omelet

Huevos Mexicanos

Baked Huevos Rancheros

Huevos à la Yucatán

Portobello Frittata

Feta and Olive Frittata

Greens, Eggs, and Ham

Goldie Lox Breakfast Burrito

Egg-in-a-Hole

Crabby Eggs Benedict

Homemade Sage and Pepper Sausage

Hash Brown Fauxtatoes

Peaches and Cream Power Shake

Coconut Power Tonic

Red, White, and Blueberry Power Shake

Cocomocha Breakfast Tonic

Yogurt Berry Power Cup

Hi-Pro Almond Yogurt Cream Spread

◇　◇　◇

◇　◇　◇

Long and unfairly maligned by the low-fat crowd because of its cholesterol content, the egg has made a strong market resurgence in recent years. And we couldn't be happier. We love eggs done almost any way and served at any time of day. We make late-night scrambles after the theater or a concert, inspired by whatever veggies or meat we happen to have on hand. We relish having a fluffy Omelet Caprese on a lazy Sunday morning and often serve Crabby Eggs Benedict for weekend brunches. Inexpensive and versatile, the incredible, edible egg is nature's prepackaged high-protein, low-carb, good-fat bargain; we believe it deserves to be returned to a place of honor in the kitchen.

Eggs are a bargain, sure, but a healthy one? You bet. As our patients and readers of our books will know, dietary cholesterol is not, nor was it ever, the health hazard it was claimed to be. Our own bodies make the lion's share of the cholesterol that circulates in our bloodstreams; the cholesterol we eat makes up a paltry 15 percent or so of the total amount. This fact has become more widely recognized even by the makers of cholesterol-reducing medications—you know the one: cholesterol comes from fried eggs and from your Uncle Joe. And to an extent that's true; however, if all is working normally metabolically, when we eat more cholesterol, preset metabolic controls kick in to reduce the amount we make, and vice versa. That is not to say that we can eat all we want of anything we want and still stay slim and healthy. If we eat a lot of cholesterol, a lot of fat, *and* a lot of carbohydrate—the all-American high-everything diet—we'll be rewarded with obesity and failing health. But, as study after study has proven, for most people, in the absence of excess amounts of starch, sugar, and high-fructose corn syrup—a carb-conscious diet—dietary cholesterol, such as you would find in eggs or a natural pork sausage patty, is not a promoter of cardiovascular risk. On a low-carb diet, eating cholesterol, from eggs or elsewhere, will not make your cholesterol rise, with one exception: damaged or oxidized cholesterol—now there's a health hazard. Oxidizing cholesterol turns it from a healthy raw material required for normal hormonal, brain, and nervous system maintenance and function into a health menace. That's why we say it's a bit better for you to keep the yolks of eggs intact when you can—in other words, poaching, coddling, frying over easy, or loosely scrambling, rather than scrambling them until they're hard and dry. The same line of reasoning leads us to recommend that you avoid eating or cooking with powdered whole eggs, dried egg yolks (not dried egg whites, which don't contain cholesterol), and all commercially prepared products containing them.

Obviously, there's not a lot of low-carb kitchen magic involved in cooking eggs; most such recipes are already low-carb as traditionally prepared. We have been able to adapt a few traditionally higher-carb preparations, such as Baked Huevos Rancheros, into carb-friendly versions through the use of black soybeans and low-carb tortillas. If you're a fan of this South of the Border classic, we think you'll be pleased with the taste. We love it as well as the Huevos à la Yucatán, which recalls the flavors of the Yucatán-inspired Huevos Motulenos we have enjoyed over the years at Pascual's, one of our favorite restaurants in Santa Fe. Their version isn't carb friendly, but boy, is it a delicious way to spend a dietary vacation.

For the most part, you'll find here a collection of some of the more interesting and unusual egg dishes among our favorites, as well as our impressions of egg preparations we've enjoyed (and still daydream of) at restaurants all over the world. We hope you'll use them as a starting point to create inspired egg dishes of your own, secure in the knowledge that eating your eggs—any time of day—really is good for you.

For those days when you're simply too pressed for time to enjoy a hot breakfast—which, for many of us, is most mornings nowadays—you'll find a collection of morning quick starts in this chapter as well. Although hectic schedules leave us little time in the morning for a meal, breaking the overnight fast with a nutritious serving of protein and good fat is imperative to good health and productivity for adults as well as kids. We keep a batch of Coconut Power Tonic in the refrigerator and on many mornings we have just enough time to pour a cup for the road. Other days, we stir together a Yogurt Berry Power Cup for a quick meal.

What we eat in the morning sets the tone for the rest of the day. Starting out, as many kids do, with a nutritionally impoverished bowlful of high-fructose corn syrup–sweetened starch (even if it's in interesting shapes with colorful characters on the box and has vitamins added to it) will lead to a blood sugar slump in the middle of the morning, a case of the heavy eyelid during math or spelling or a ten o'clock meeting, and a gnawing hunger before lunch—not exactly a recipe for success for kids or parents. Excellence in nutrition should be every morning's goal. A nourishing breakfast—even a quick one—that's rich in protein and good quality fats will keep your mind sharper and your hunger at bay longer.

Omelet Caprese

SERVES 1

The flavors of the southern coast of Italy—tomatoes, basil, and fresh mozzarella—combine in this delicious dish. It's a filling meal in an omelet pan, but we love to round it out with some slices of ripe melon wrapped in prosciutto or a few strips of crisp bacon and a serving of berries on the side. To save time, double the recipe, make it in a larger skillet, and cut it in half to serve two.

Protein per serving:
29 grams

Effective carb per serving:
4.4 grams

3 eggs
salt and pepper to taste
1 ounce fresh mozzarella
½ Roma (or small red) tomato
2 or 3 leaves fresh basil
1 tablespoon unsalted butter
1 tablespoon chopped onion
few drops balsamic vinegar
1 tablespoon sour cream

Beat the eggs thoroughly with salt and pepper.

Dice the mozzarella and tomato and set aside.

Slice two leaves of basil into thin strips, leaving one leaf whole for the garnish.

Melt the butter in an omelet pan or a small skillet over medium-high heat.

Sauté the onion until transparent.

Add the beaten eggs and allow to set slightly, then lift the edges to permit the uncooked egg to slide beneath the cooked until no liquid egg remains.

Scatter the diced cheese and tomatoes and the strips of basil onto the top of the omelet. Allow the cheese to begin to melt.

Fold the omelet in half and slide onto a serving plate.

Top with the basil leaf, the balsamic vinegar, and the sour cream.

Farmer's Veggie Omelet

SERVES 4

A complete meal in a pan, this omelet has it all. We love the combination of broccoli, mushroom, and cheddar, but you could also substitute a cup and a half other low-carb veggies, such as zucchini, yellow squash, bell peppers, asparagus, tomatoes, or cauliflower, as you like.

Protein per serving:
19 grams

Effective carb per serving:
3.9 grams

1 cup fresh or frozen broccoli florets
1 tablespoon olive oil
1 tablespoon butter
1 small red onion, sliced
½ cup fresh mushrooms or 1 can (4 ounces) sliced mushrooms, drained
1 tablespoon minced fresh parsley or 1 teaspoon dried*
1 tablespoon minced fresh basil or 1 teaspoon dried
1 teaspoon fines herbes
¼ teaspoon salt
¼ teaspoon freshly ground black pepper
8 large eggs
¾ cup shredded cheddar cheese

Preheat the oven to 350 degrees.

Slice the broccoli florets lengthwise to make pieces of similar size. If using frozen broccoli, thaw and drain first.

Heat the oil and butter in an ovenproof skillet over medium heat. Sauté the onion until translucent, add the broccoli and mushrooms, and cook for another minute or two, stirring often. Add the herbs, salt, and pepper.

In a separate bowl, beat the eggs and add half of the cheese.

Pour the egg mixture into the skillet and stir to combine with the vegetables.

Cook for a few minutes on the stove top to set the bottom, then top with the remaining cheese.

Bake in the oven for 12 to 15 minutes until the eggs are set and the cheese is golden brown.

Cut into quarters and serve immediately.

*Soak dried herbs in 1 tablespoon of water for a few minutes beforehand; drain any excess water before using.

Huevos Mexicanos

SERVES 2

This recipe recalls the great times we've spent sitting with our bare feet in the sand in a beachfront café in Zihuatenejo, Mexico, and digging into a piping hot plate of eggs à la Mexicana after a long morning walk beside the ocean. The venue may be different, but the flavors are right on.

Protein per serving:
37 grams

Effective carb per serving:
5.5 grams

PICO DE GALLO
1 Roma (or small red) tomato, seeded and diced
¼ red onion, peeled and diced
½ Serrano pepper, seeded and finely minced
1 tablespoon chopped fresh cilantro
¼ teaspoon salt
½ lime, juice only

EGGS
5 eggs
½ cup shredded Mexican cheese blend or shredded cheddar
½ teaspoon ground cumin
¼ teaspoon salt
¼ teaspoon freshly ground black pepper
1 tablespoon unsalted butter

In a small bowl, make the pico de gallo by mixing the diced tomato, onion, pepper, cilantro, salt, and lime juice. Set aside.

Beat the eggs until light yellow.

Add the cheese, cumin, salt, and pepper.

Heat the butter in a skillet. When foamy, pour in the egg mixture and gently scramble until cooked.

Top each plate with half of the pico de gallo, equally divided. Serve immediately.

Baked Huevos Rancheros

SERVES 6

This easy version of the classic dish will let you enjoy that slow-cooked bean and tortilla taste that travelers to Mexico and the American Southwest have come to love. The best part is, you can do it without investing all day or breaking your carb bank.

Protein per serving:
29 grams

Effective carb per serving:
11.6 grams

6 small low-carb tortillas (taco size)
¾ cup rinsed and drained black soybeans
1½ cups shredded Mexican cheese (divided in half for use)
1 small can (4 ounces) diced green chili peppers
1 can (14 ounces) diced roasted tomatoes, drained
1 teaspoon dried cumin
1 teaspoon salt
½ teaspoon freshly ground black pepper
12 tablespoons canned red or green chile enchilada sauce, hot or mild
12 large eggs
2 tablespoons minced fresh cilantro

Preheat the oven to 350 degrees.

Generously grease a 6-cup (large) muffin tin with coconut oil or line with parchment.

Place one tortilla into each cup and press down to make a bowl. Trim the excess to prevent the edges from becoming too crisp.

In a small saucepan, mix the black soybeans with half of the cheese, the green chilies, tomatoes, cumin, salt, and pepper. Stir to combine.

Over medium heat, cook the mixture for 10 to 15 minutes, until it begins to thicken and the beans start to break apart. Encourage this by smashing a few.

Divide the bean mixture evenly among the 6 cups and top each with 1 tablespoon of the enchilada sauce.

Crack 2 eggs into each cup. Top with the remaining cheese, dividing equally among the cups. Spoon 1 tablespoon of the remaining enchilada sauce over each cup.

Bake for about 25 minutes until the whites are set.

(If you like your yolks runny, separate the yolks from the whites. Place the whites only atop the bean mixture, reserving the yolks in an oiled bowl. Bake for about 20 minutes to set the whites, remove from the oven, slip 2 yolks atop the beans in each cup, top with cheese, and bake for an additional 5 to 7 minutes.)

Allow the eggs to cool slightly, remove them from the muffin tin to plates, top with cilantro, and serve.

Huevos à la Yucatán

SERVES 6

The flavors of sun-drenched Mexico will fill your mouth when you make this easy and lower-carb version of Huevos Motulenos. You can almost taste the tropics in the black soybeans, smoky cumin, bright cilantro, and hot chiles. The traditional dish is usually made with diced bacon, pork, or ham, and you could certainly add those if you'd like. This version, however, would be suitable for entertaining even your vegetarian friends.

Protein per serving:
29 grams

Effective carb per serving:
11.3 grams

1 small banana
1 teaspoon coconut oil
6 small low-carb tortillas (taco size)
¾ cup rinsed and drained black soybeans
1½ cups shredded Mexican cheese (divided in half for use)
1 small can (4 ounces) diced green chili peppers
1 teaspoon dried cumin
1 teaspoon salt
½ teaspoon freshly ground black pepper
12 tablespoons canned green chile enchilada sauce, hot or mild
12 large eggs
2 tablespoons minced fresh cilantro

Preheat the oven to 350 degrees.

Slice the banana on the diagonal into 12 oval slices.

In a small skillet, melt the coconut oil. Sauté the banana slices just until they begin to soften. Set aside.

Lightly oil a 6-cup (large) muffin tin with coconut oil or line with parchment.

Place 1 tortilla into each cup and press down to make a bowl. Trim the excess to prevent the edges from becoming too crisp.

In a small bowl, mix the black soybeans with half of the cheese, the green chilies, cumin, salt, and pepper. Stir to combine.

Divide the bean mixture evenly among the 6 cups and top each with 1 tablespoon of the enchilada sauce.

Place 2 banana slices atop the beans in each cup.

Crack 2 eggs into each cup. Top with the remaining cheese,

dividing equally among the cups. Spoon 1 tablespoon of the remaining enchilada sauce over each cup.

Bake for about 25 minutes until the whites are set.

(If you like your yolks runny, separate the yolks from the whites. Place the whites only atop the bean mixture, reserving the yolks in an oiled bowl. Bake for about 20 minutes to set the whites, remove from the oven, slip 2 yolks atop the beans in each muffin cup, top with cheese, and bake for an additional 5 to 7 minutes.)

Allow the eggs to cool slightly, remove them from the muffin tin to plates, top with cilantro, and serve.

Portobello Frittata

This savory egg dish makes a beautiful presentation for a brunch or even a lunch gathering, but it's easy enough to make anytime and chock-full of protein, good fats, and folate. Frittatas are also a great way to use up either whites or yolks left over from other recipes. You can substitute a couple of egg whites or a couple of yolks in place of up to two of the whole eggs called for.

Protein per serving:
17.5 grams

Effective carb per serving:
4.2 grams

6 eggs
1 package (10 ounces) frozen chopped spinach, thawed
1 cup ricotta cheese
¾ cup freshly grated Parmigiano Reggiano*
¼ teaspoon dried basil
¼ teaspoon oregano
¼ teaspoon garlic
coarse salt and freshly ground black pepper to taste
¾ cup chopped portobello mushrooms
4 green onions, chopped (white and some green parts)
1 tablespoon unsalted butter

Preheat the oven to 375 degrees.
    In a large bowl, beat the eggs.
    Add all the ingredients except the mushrooms, onions, and butter to the eggs; stir to thoroughly combine the cheeses and spices.
    In an ovenproof skillet, sauté the portobello pieces and chopped onions in butter for a minute or so, just to wilt.
    Add the egg mixture to the skillet; stir carefully to combine.
    Bake for 25 to 30 minutes until set.
    Cool for 15 to 20 minutes, cut into 6 wedges, and serve.

*You can save grating time, if you wish, by purchasing pregrated Parmigiano Reggiano. Freshly grated cheese has a more intense flavor, however.

Feta and Olive Frittata

SERVES 4 AS A
MEAL OR 8 AS
AN APPETIZER

We love to travel in Greece and can't get enough of the delicious olives and cheeses (and tart local wines) when we're there. This simple frittata draws on those flavors. It's great for breakfast with a side of sausage or bacon and some fruit but easily makes the transition to brunch or lunch. Pair it with a salad of chunked tomatoes, cucumbers, onions, and a tasty vinaigrette as a main course or an appetizer.

As a Meal

Protein per serving:
12.4 grams

Effective carb per serving:
2.8 grams

As an Appetizer

Protein per serving:
6.2 grams

Effective carb per serving:
1.4 grams

6 whole eggs or 3 eggs plus 4 whites
½ cup crumbled feta cheese
10 to 12 kalamata olives, pitted and sliced
¼ teaspoon salt
¼ teaspoon freshly ground black pepper
2 tablespoons butter

GARNISH
1 tablespoon sour cream
1 tablespoon minced fresh flat-leaf parsley

Preheat the oven to 350 degrees.

In a bowl, beat the eggs and mix in the cheese, olives, salt, and pepper.

In an ovenproof skillet, nonstick if possible, melt the butter over medium heat until foamy.

Pour the egg mixture into the skillet, reduce the heat to medium-low, and let it cook undisturbed for about 10 minutes until the bottom is firm.

Place the skillet into the oven and bake for 10 to 20 more minutes until the top is no longer runny. Check every 5 minutes or so to prevent burning.

When fully set, remove the skillet from the oven, loosen the frittata gently from the bottom with a flexible spatula, slide onto a serving plate, garnish with a dollop of sour cream, and sprinkle all over with parsley. Serve immediately or allow to cool and serve at room temperature.

You can also allow the frittata to cool, wrap it in plastic wrap, and refrigerate it for up to 24 hours. To serve, remove the plastic and gently reheat in a warm (200-degree) oven for 10 minutes or so.

Greens, Eggs, and Ham

SERVES 2

We love egg scrambles any time of the day, and we seem to make them in endless varieties. This one, with apologies to Dr. Seuss, is a favorite combo and a delicious way to get a load of vitamins and minerals such as folate, beta-carotene, and potassium along with enough protein to see you through the busiest day.

Protein per serving:
34 grams

Effective carb per serving:
4.7 grams

1 tablespoon olive oil
1 tablespoon butter
¼ onion, diced
1 clove garlic, minced or pressed
2 cups fresh spinach leaves
6 eggs
salt and pepper to taste
4 ounces cooked ham or Canadian bacon, diced
2 ounces cream cheese, cut into ½-inch cubes

Heat the olive oil and butter in a skillet until foamy. Sauté the onion and garlic until translucent; do not burn.

Add the spinach leaves and sauté for a minute or two, just to wilt.

In a bowl, beat the eggs.

Add the salt, pepper, diced ham, and cream cheese cubes.

Add the egg mixture to the sautéed ingredients in the skillet and cook over medium to medium-high heat, gently turning the eggs as the cheese melts. Serve immediately.

Goldie Lox Breakfast Burrito

SERVES 2

We devised these quick breakfast burritos in happy recollection of the scrambled-egg dish we've enjoyed often at Sarabeth's, one of our favorite spots for breakfast in New York. Whether you choose to wrap it in a tortilla for a portable meal or serve it on a plate with a side of fruit or a salad, we're sure, like Goldie herself, you'll say it's just right.

Protein per serving:
35.7 grams

Effective carb per serving:
9.4 grams

2 large (wrap size) low-carb tortillas
4 eggs
2 green onions, diced (green and white parts)
2 ounces cream cheese, cubed and softened
4 ounces lox (or smoked salmon), diced
¼ teaspoon salt
¼ teaspoon freshly ground black pepper
1 tablespoon butter
1 tablespoon rinsed and drained capers

Prepare the tortillas for warming—roll each tortilla in a paper towel and set aside.

In a bowl, beat the eggs well and add all the remaining ingredients, except the butter and capers, stirring to combine.

Melt the butter in a skillet over medium heat. When it foams, add the egg mixture and cook over medium-low heat, gently and occasionally scrambling to prevent burning, just until the eggs are no longer wet and the cheese has melted.

While the eggs cook, warm the rolled tortillas in the microwave for 30 seconds each.*

At the last moment, stir the capers into the eggs and remove the eggs from the heat.

Divide the eggs between the two warmed tortillas, roll up, and serve with a dollop of sour cream or a dash of Tabasco sauce, if desired.

*If you do not have a microwave, warm the tortillas on the stovetop. Lay them flat in a pan over a low flame for a few minutes, flipping often with tongs to prevent burning.

Egg-in-a-Hole

SERVES 1

This recipe owes its origin to the much-beloved cook at our son's college fraternity house. An entire generation of frat members started their day off right with a couple of Leon's Eggs-in-a-Hole, and many, like our son, brought the technique home. It's a no muss, no fuss, all-in-one breakfast that never fails to make us think fondly of Leon.

Protein per serving:
10.3 grams

Effective carb per serving:
5.6 grams
(depending on the bread you use)

1 pat butter
1 slice commercial low-carb bread
1 egg
salt and pepper to taste

Lightly butter both sides of the bread.

With a biscuit cutter or a round cookie cutter, cut a 2-inch circle from the center of the slice of bread.

Heat a skillet or a griddle over medium-high heat.

Place the bread slice and center circle into the skillet or onto the griddle.

Break the egg into the hole, sprinkle with salt and pepper, and fry until the white is set.

Flip the egg and toasted bread circle and cook briefly to the desired level, 10 to 15 seconds for over easy or 20 to 30 seconds for a firm yolk.

Remove to a serving plate and eat immediately. Enjoy the toast circle with a bit of low-carb jam or fruit. (Be sure to count the extra carbs if you add jam.)

Crabby Eggs Benedict

SERVES 4

This is a whole different and wonderful take on the classic egg dish and one that we enjoy for breakfast, brunch, lunch, or even a late-night light supper. It's a great use for leftover crab cakes— although at our place we'd have to make a double batch of those to have leftovers. All you'll need to make it a meal is a side of fruit, a sliced fresh tomato, or Mixed Greens with Spicy Lime Vinaigrette (page 94). Okay, and maybe some champagne.

Protein per serving:
45 grams
(This is a hearty meal; smaller appetites will do fine with a half portion.)

Effective carb per serving:
6.7 grams

1 recipe Easy Blender Hollandaise Sauce (page 170)
8 small crab cakes, cooked*
8 eggs
1 tablespoon white wine vinegar

Prepare the hollandaise sauce as per the recipe and have it ready.

Keep the crab cakes warm (or warm up leftover ones) in a 200-degree oven as you proceed.

Poach the eggs by whatever method you choose. One method is slipping them in a large pan of simmering to barely boiling water to which you've added the vinegar. Do this carefully, one at a time. Cook them about 3 minutes or to the desired level of doneness—for us that's whites totally set but yolks still runny.

When the eggs are done, place two crab cakes on each plate, top each with a poached egg, and pour a generous dollop of hollandaise sauce over each one. Serve immediately.

*You can make 8 small crab cakes from 1 recipe of Crab Cakes, page 134.

Homemade Sage and Pepper Sausage

SERVES 8

Although it may be something you've never thought to do, making your own patty sausage takes only minutes and ensures that it's made with top-quality meat and contains no fillers, preservatives, flavor enhancers, or hidden sources of carbohydrate. The added benefit is that you can flavor your sausage to your liking by altering the amounts of sage, spices, or heat. It takes only a bit longer to make a double or triple batch, and doing so saves time in the long run.

Protein per serving:
14.4 grams

Effective carb per serving:
0.3 gram

1 teaspoon freshly ground black pepper
1 teaspoon rubbed sage
½ teaspoon onion powder
¼ teaspoon dried thyme
¼ teaspoon cayenne pepper*
⅛ teaspoon ground ginger
1 packet Splenda
1½ pounds ground pork, turkey, or chicken

Mix all the spices together in a ziplock bag.

Add the spice mixture to the ground pork (or turkey or chicken) and knead briefly to combine.

Form the sausage mixture into a log 2 to 3 inches in diameter and wrap it tightly in plastic wrap.

Refrigerate overnight, if possible, to enhance the flavor.

Cut the sausage into ½-inch rounds and press into thin patties for frying.

To freeze, place the patties separately on a baking sheet and freeze overnight. Store in ziplock freezer bags for individual use. The sausages will keep frozen for up to 6 months. Thaw them before frying.

*For hotter sausage, add up to ½ teaspoon cayenne or ½ to 1 teaspoon crushed red pepper flakes.

Hash Brown Fauxtatoes

SERVES 4

These impostors have all the flavor and texture of the original article—maybe even more so—but many fewer carbs thanks to our old friend the celery root. They're best when fried in bacon drippings (grease), but olive oil will work fine. Throw a few strips of bacon and a couple of fried eggs beside them on the plate, add a bowl of berries and melon on the side, and you've got yourself a hearty start to any day. To save time, make extra; they reheat just fine for the next day or two.

Protein per serving:
2.5 grams

Effective carb per serving:
12.4 grams

1 large celery root, trimmed and peeled
1 teaspoon plus ½ teaspoon salt (divided for use)
2 tablespoons olive oil or bacon grease
1 clove garlic, peeled and minced
1 small sweet onion, peeled and diced small
½ red bell pepper, seeded and diced small
½ green bell pepper, seeded and diced small
½ teaspoon freshly ground black pepper

Dice the celery root small, into about ¼-inch pieces.

Place the pieces into a medium saucepan, cover with water, add 1 teaspoon of the salt, cover, and bring to a boil. Cook for 5 or 6 minutes to soften. Drain well.

Meanwhile, heat the olive oil in a heavy skillet over medium heat. Sauté the garlic, onion, and peppers until limp.

Add the celery root and continue to cook undisturbed for 2 minutes or so to let the pieces caramelize a bit. Season with the remaining salt and the pepper; stir and toss to distribute. Continue to cook long enough to brown the other side.

Serve immediately or hold, covered, in a warm (200-degree) oven for up to 30 minutes.

Peaches and Cream Power Shake

SERVES 4

Cool, refreshing, sweet, and lightly peachy, this is a quick morning breakfast you'll love when there's no time to cook. It's perfect for a small protein requirement; bigger appetites may want to stir an additional scoop of vanilla (or strawberry) protein powder into their serving to boost the protein sufficiently to make a meal. In peach season, make it with fresh peaches and blend in a few ice cubes to thicken it.

Protein per serving:
21.9 grams

Effective carb per serving:
6 grams

½ cup frozen, unsweetened sliced peaches, thawed
1 can (14.5 ounces) premium unsweetened coconut milk
1½ cups water
3 eggs, beaten
60 grams (about 3 scoops) vanilla-flavored low-carb whey protein powder
8 packets Splenda
pinch salt (or to taste)

In a blender or a food processor, puree the peaches until smooth.

In a saucepan, place the coconut milk, water, beaten eggs, whey protein powder, Splenda, and salt; whisk to mix well.

Gently cook over medium heat, stirring constantly, until the mixture begins to thicken and will coat the back of a spoon.

Remove from the heat and stir in the peach puree.

Pour the shake mixture into a covered pitcher or bowl and cool quickly by half submerging the container into an ice-water bath and stirring until the temperature drops.

Store, tightly sealed, in the refrigerator for up to 4 days.

Serve chilled in 8-ounce portions for a quick breakfast or in 1-ounce shooters as a brunch appetizer.

Coconut Power Tonic

SERVES 4

No time to eat breakfast? Posh! If you need a breakfast that's ready to go in the morning, whip up a big batch of this power tonic for a glass of thick and creamy nutrition on the run. The coconut milk contains lauric acid, an immune-boosting fat; the dolomite powder packs in calcium and magnesium for strong bones; and the eggs and whey protein powder provide plenty of protein. Quick, healthy, and delicious.

Protein per serving:
20.6 grams
(You can increase the protein content per serving by adding scoops of low-carb whey protein powder if your per-meal protein requirement is significantly higher.)

Effective carb per serving:
3.5 grams

1 can (14.5 ounces) premium unsweetened coconut milk
2 cups water
4 eggs, well beaten
3 scoops vanilla whey protein powder
1 teaspoon dolomite powder*
pinch salt (or to taste)
1 teaspoon pure vanilla extract
4 packets Splenda (optional)

In a saucepan, whisk together all the ingredients until well blended.

Cook over medium-low heat, stirring constantly, until the mixture begins to thicken slightly and will coat the back of a spoon.

Remove from the heat and cool quickly by half submerging the pan in an ice-water bath, stirring constantly.

When cool, pour the power tonic into a pitcher with a tight-fitting lid and store in the refrigerator for up to 4 days.

*Dolomite powder is a natural calcium and magnesium supplement available at most health food grocers and vitamin shops or online.

Red, White, and Blueberry Power Shake

SERVES 1

This shake is not only patriotic, it's chock-full of healthful anti-oxidants, immune boosters, and protein to boot. For a different twist, make it a New Mexican Sunrise shake with a quarter cup each of pureed unsweetened peaches on top and pureed raspberries on the bottom. Any low-sugar fruit will work, and kids of all ages can have fun mixing and matching the colors. Kiwi and blueberries, anyone?

Protein per serving:
23.8 grams

Effective carb per serving:
9.4 grams
(This carb value is for raspberries and blueberries. Selecting different fruits will alter the counts but not markedly so.)

1 cup fresh (or frozen unsweetened, thawed) blueberries (divided for use)
2 packets Splenda (optional)
1 cup fresh (or frozen unsweetened, thawed) raspberries (divided for use)
8 ounces Coconut Power Tonic (page 50)
½ cup crushed ice (or an amount sufficient to thicken the shake)

In a blender, puree 1 cup of the blueberries with 1 packet of Splenda (if desired) until smooth.

Pour into a clean storage container with an airtight lid and refrigerate until ready to use.

Rinse the blender and repeat steps 1 and 2 with the raspberries.

In a clean blender, combine the Coconut Power Tonic and the ice and blend on high speed until thick. Add more ice to increase the thickness, if desired.

For each serving desired, pour ¼ cup of the blueberry puree into the bottom of a tall glass. Refrigerate the remainder for future use.

Carefully pour in the thickened Coconut Power Tonic.

Gently float ¼ cup of the raspberry puree on top. Refrigerate the remainder for future use.

Cocomocha Breakfast Tonic

SERVES 4

Chocolate, coffee, and coconut sound good to start your day? This low-carb version of a frozen cappuccino comes with an immune-system-enhancing boost from the coconut milk and a protein kick. It's a breakfast drink so rich and filling that it will make you forget all about your extra-large, six-pump, white chocolate frozen mocha.

Protein per serving:
21.9 grams

Effective carb per serving:
4 grams

3 eggs, beaten
1 can (14.5 ounces) premium unsweetened coconut milk
2 cups strong coffee, caffeinated or decaffeinated
60 grams (about 3 scoops) chocolate-flavored whey protein powder
4 packets Splenda
1 teaspoon dolomite powder*
pinch salt (or to taste)

In a saucepan, place the eggs, coconut milk, coffee, whey protein powder, Splenda, dolomite powder, and salt; whisk to mix well.

Gently cook over medium heat, stirring constantly, until the mixture begins to thicken and will coat the back of a spoon.

Remove from the heat and cool quickly by half submerging the pan in an ice-water bath, stirring constantly.

When cool, pour the breakfast tonic into a pitcher with a tight-fitting lid and store in the refrigerator for up to 4 days.

Serve chilled in 8-ounce portions for a quick breakfast or an afternoon pick-me-up snack. If desired, blend the tonic with crushed ice until smooth and thick for a frozen mocha treat.

*Dolomite powder is a natural calcium and magnesium supplement available at most health food grocers and vitamin shops or online.

Yogurt Berry Power Cup

SERVES 4

If you crave the creamy sweetness of commercial fruit-flavored yogurt but hate the slug of high-fructose corn syrup that sweetens most products, you'll love this quick and easy recipe. It makes a great after-school snack for kids, a quick breakfast, or a protein, fruit, and calcium fix for kids of all ages.

Protein per serving:
24.8 grams

Effective carb per serving:
14 grams

16 ounces plain, unsweetened yogurt (organic if possible)

2 cups fresh or frozen unsweetened mixed berries

2 packets Splenda or stevia (optional)

4 scoops (about 80 grams) vanilla or strawberry low-carb whey protein powder

Line a 2-cup mesh strainer with a paper coffee filter and place the strainer over a mixing bowl sufficiently large to suspend it and catch the filtered liquid.

Fill the filter with the yogurt, cover it with a clean cloth or waxed paper, and set the strainer-bowl in the refrigerator for several hours, during which time much of the liquid trapped in the yogurt will drain into the bowl and the yogurt will thicken considerably.

Meanwhile, in a blender or a food processor, puree the berries with the sweetener and protein powder and refrigerate until ready to use.

When ready, place the thickened yogurt into a mixing bowl and stir in the berry puree, mixing thoroughly.

Serve in 8-ounce portions. Store the remainder, tightly covered, in the refrigerator for up to 3 days.

Hi-Pro Almond Yogurt Cream Spread

**MAKES 16
TABLESPOONS**

This spread makes a higher protein, lower calorie replacement for cream cheese. You can use it as a topping for low-carb toast or low-carb bagels in the morning for a change of pace. It is delicious, too, on warm low-carb tortillas. The secret is to let as much of the liquid as possible drain from the yogurt.

*Protein per
tablespoon:*
3.4 grams

*Effective carb
per tablespoon:*
1.1 grams

8 ounces plain, unsweetened yogurt
2 scoops (about 40 grams) natural flavor low-carb whey protein powder
2 packets Splenda or stevia
1 teaspoon almond extract
¼ cup finely chopped sliced almonds

In a bowl, thoroughly combine the yogurt, protein powder, sweetener, almond extract, and chopped almonds.

Line a 2-cup mesh strainer with a paper coffee filter and place the strainer over a mixing bowl sufficiently large to suspend it and catch the filtered liquid.*

Fill the filter with the yogurt, cover it with a clean cloth or waxed paper, and set the strainer-bowl in the refrigerator at least overnight, during which time almost all of the liquid trapped in the yogurt will drain into the bowl and the yogurt will attain the consistency of cream cheese.

When the draining is complete, turn the finished product out into a clean container with a tight-fitting lid and store in the refrigerator for up to a week.

*If you enjoy making your own cream cheese alternatives and make these recipes often, you might wish to invest in a ready-made yogurt strainer/yogurt cheese maker, which you can find online.

CHAPTER 3

◇ ◇ ◇

Appetizers and Savory Breads

Asian Spiced Pecans

Avocado-Caviar Spoons

Cucumber-Salmon Bites

Black Soybean Hummus

Caribbean Black Soybean Salsa

Salsa Verde (Roasted Green Tomatillo Salsa)

Blue Cheese Lorraine Miniatures

Spicy Tortilla Triangles

Parmesan Crisps

Cheesy Waffle Pizza Platforms

Country Corn Bread

Cornmeal Johnnycakes

Garlic Parmesan Griddle Bread

Handmade Rye Bread

Rosemary and Olive Pan Bread

◇ ◇ ◇

◇　◇　◇

Getting together with friends for a dinner party or drinks and hors d'oeuvres can sometimes prove a disastrous temptation to stray from a low-carb diet. Every canapé must have its bread or cracker platform, every dip must have its chip. Although many salsa and cream cheese dips are naturally low in carb, the dippers usually aren't. And some dips—hummus, which we dearly love, comes immediately to mind—are no real carb bargain themselves before even taking into account the warm pita triangle or tortilla chip needed to scoop them up. Sure, we carb-conscious dieters can nibble on cheese, meats, pickled vegetables, olives, and nuts; sure we can enjoy a shrimp cocktail or oysters on the half shell before dinner; and just as surely there's got to be more.

Indeed, there is more, and you'll find some new options here. In this chapter, we've included recipes for elegant hors d'oeuvres such as Avocado-Caviar Spoons and the casual ones such as Caribbean Black Soybean Salsa; you'll find spicy in our Spicy Tortilla Triangles and Salsa Verde and savory in the Blue Cheese Lorraine Miniatures. Here you'll find our reduced-carb version of Black Soybean Hummus, and if you're a fan of the original, you many feel, as we did, that the long dry spell is over.

In addition, you'll find a selection of carb-reduced savory breads that will please even your nondieting friends. We love to serve the casual Cornmeal Johnnycakes alongside soups, stews, chili, and chowders because they can be made ahead of time and kept warm for easy soup, salad, and bread dinners. But our all-time favorite is the

Rosemary and Olive Pan Bread; it's a feast for the eye and a treat to the palate. We enjoy it alongside Spanish or Mediterranean dishes or even in bite-size pieces as a part of a tray of antipasti with wine.

The low-carb magic in these savory breads comes, as it does for most of our baked goods, primarily from replacing most or all of the wheat flour or cornmeal of the original with almond flour and some of the impostor ingredients that help it to behave more like wheat flour. (You'll find more about them in the introduction to chapter 1.) Also, by replacing higher-carb beans, such as garbanzo beans and black turtle beans, with the versatile black soybean (which is much higher in protein and fiber and lower in usable carbohydrates than its relatives), you'll be able to create tasty, filling, and very nutritious appetizers and savory breads that will please your family, your friends, and your waistline.

Asian Spiced Pecans

MAKES ABOUT
24 (1-OUNCE)
SERVINGS

Easy, tasty, and far cheaper than their commercially available compadres, these nuts are great as a spicy appetizer, with coffee after dinner, scattered over salads, or in the case of sweeter combinations, mixed into low-carb ice cream. Any spice combination you enjoy will work as long as the spices combine happily, and that's pretty much a matter of your own tastes. We've offered two of our favorites here—one savory and one sweet.

Garlic

Protein per serving:
2.6 grams

Effective carb per serving:
1.5 grams

Ginger

Protein per serving:
2.6 grams

Effective carb per serving:
2.2 grams

GARLIC SPICE BLEND
2 tablespoons garlic salt
2 tablespoons freshly ground black pepper
2 tablespoons paprika
2 tablespoons Japanese Dashi

GINGER SPICE BLEND
2 tablespoons ground ginger
2 tablespoons paprika
6 tablespoons granular Splenda
1 teaspoon cayenne pepper (or to taste)
2 egg whites
3 cups pecan halves

Preheat the oven to 225 degrees.

In a ziplock bag, combine all the ingredients of either the garlic spice blend or the ginger spice blend. Shake well to combine.

Lightly beat the egg whites.

Toss the nuts in the egg whites and roll each one in your choice of the spice blend.

Spread the pecans out on a parchment-lined baking sheet and bake for 10 to 15 minutes.

Let the nuts cool and put them into a jar or a ziplock bag.

Avocado-Caviar Spoons

**SERVES 8
(MAKES ABOUT
16 SPOONS)**

When the evening calls for a splash of elegance, whether as a little surprise treat before the first dinner course or as an appetizer with drinks on a more formal evening, try these luscious little bites. They're quick and easy to make, look quite impressive, and make a little bit of caviar go a long way. This calls for inexpensive whitefish caviar, which for this recipe is just fine. Save the pricey Beluga and Osetra to savor all by themselves on a beautiful small spoon.

*Protein per
serving:*
1.4 grams

*Effective carb
per serving:*
0.8 gram

1 recipe Mexican Cream (page 171)
1 small jar (about 2 ounces) black whitefish caviar
1 lemon (divided in half for use)
1 large ripe Haas avocado

Prepare the Mexican Cream.

Drain the caviar into a fine mesh strainer, rinse with water, and drain again. Put the caviar into a small bowl and squeeze the juice of half a lemon directly over it and set aside.

Halve, seed, and slice the avocado halves across from side to side into 4 slices. Slice each in half lengthwise to create 16 bite-size pieces.

Squeeze the juice of the other half of the lemon over the avocado pieces.

Drain the excess lemon juice from the caviar and gently separate the caviar with a spoon.

Place one piece of avocado on each of 16 pretty teaspoons and top with a teaspoon of the Mexican Cream and with a sprinkling or more of caviar to your liking.

Cucumber-Salmon Bites

MAKES 32
PIECES

Tasty, refreshing, and light, these appetizers are easy enough to serve often and pretty enough for a party. And they're so easy on the carb budget that you can eat your fill guilt-free. Although the recipe doesn't call for it, they'd be even prettier with a sprinkling of red caviar in place of the black olive slice.

Protein per piece:
1 gram

Effective carb per piece:
0.4 gram

2 large English cucumbers, washed, unpeeled
4 ounces smoked salmon, sliced thin
4 ounces cream cheese, softened
2 tablespoons fresh flat-leaf parsley
1 teaspoon hot wasabi powder
1 tablespoon soy sauce
½ teaspoon freshly ground black pepper
32 black olive slices

Trim the ends from the cucumbers and slice each one into approximately 16 rounds, about ½ inch thick, to make 32 platforms.

Slice the salmon into 1-inch squares, reserving the oddly shaped scraps for the cheese.

In a food processor, combine the cream cheese, salmon scraps, parsley, wasabi powder, soy sauce, and pepper and blend until smooth.

To assemble the bites, top each cucumber round with a slice of salmon and a dollop of the salmon cream cheese.

Garnish each bite with a black olive slice.

Black Soybean Hummus

SERVES 8

This lower-carb version of one of our favorite Mediterranean comfort foods is not only a great appetizer, it's also a delicious and nourishing snack for kids of all ages. We reduced some of the carb of the original by replacing half the garbanzo beans with black soybeans and substituting low-carb whole-wheat tortillas for pita bread. You could reduce it even further by using all black soybeans and no chickpeas, but it would lose some of its appeal.

Protein per serving:
8.5 grams

Effective carb per serving:
13.5 grams
(Values are for the dip only and do not include tortilla or pita triangles or veggie sticks used as dippers.)

½ cup sesame seeds
¾ cup extra-virgin olive oil
1 can (15 ounces) garbanzo beans (chickpeas), rinsed and drained
1 can (15 ounces) black soybeans, rinsed and drained
2 cloves garlic
2 teaspoons cumin
1 teaspoon onion powder
1 teaspoon fine salt
1 lime, juice only
¼ teaspoon paprika (for garnish)

Toast the sesame seeds in a heavy skillet over medium heat until lightly browned, 3 or 4 minutes.

Place the seeds into a food processor, add the olive oil, and pulse to coarsely chop.

Add all the remaining ingredients, except the paprika garnish, and pulse until relatively smooth.

Place the hummus into a tightly covered container and refrigerate for several hours.

Allow the hummus to come to room temperature before serving.

Drizzle with a couple of teaspoons of good, strong Mediterranean extra-virgin olive oil, sprinkle with paprika, and enjoy with warm low-carb tortilla triangles.

Caribbean Black Soybean Salsa

SERVES 4

You'll savor the flavor of the islands when you enjoy this easy-to-prepare and delicious salsa. It's great as a side dish with fish and chicken, but equally good with Mexican or Southwestern entrees or as a dip with low-carb tortillas or chips.

Protein per serving:
8.5 grams

Effective carb per serving:
5.6 grams

1 can (14 ounces) black soybeans
1 Roma (or small red) tomato
2 to 3 green onions
½ yellow bell pepper
1 Serrano or jalapeño pepper
handful cilantro
1 lime, juice and zest
1 tablespoon extra-virgin olive oil
1 teaspoon cumin
1 teaspoon freshly ground black pepper
¼ teaspoon cayenne pepper
1 teaspoon salt

Drain and rinse the black soybeans.

Chop and seed the tomato. Chop the green onions, bell pepper, Serrano pepper, and cilantro.

Juice and zest the lime over the top.

Place all ingredients into a large bowl and mix to combine.

Cover the salsa and allow it to marinate for several hours before serving.

Salsa Verde (Roasted Green Tomatillo Salsa)

SERVES 8

This salsa is the freshest, tangiest, and tastiest tomatillo salsa we've ever found. All of its ingredients are naturally low in carb—it's the dippers that create the problem. Try dipping it with warm low-carb flour tortillas or using it warm as a sauce on chicken, fish, or pork.

Protein per serving:
1 gram

Effective carb per serving:
2.3 grams

1 teaspoon coconut oil
¾ pound whole green tomatillos, in their husks
½ small red onion, peeled and quartered
1 small Serrano pepper, stemmed and seeded
1 clove garlic, peeled
1 teaspoon freshly ground black pepper
1 tablespoon lemon juice
1 tablespoon lime juice
6 ounces water
1½ teaspoons salt
1 ripe Haas avocado
1 tablespoon freshly chopped cilantro

Lightly oil a griddle or a skillet with the coconut oil and melt it over medium-high heat.

Cook the tomatillos, onion, Serrano pepper, and garlic until they begin to brown.

Remove the tomatillos to a bowl and cover them with ice to cool.

When cool enough to handle, remove and discard the husks from the tomatillos and cut them into quarters.

Place all the cooked vegetables, black pepper, lemon and lime juices, water, and salt into a blender and blend until smooth.

Refrigerate the blended salsa, tightly covered, for several hours or up to 2 days.

Just before serving, dice the avocado and add it and the cilantro to the salsa. Pulse the salsa in a food processor a few times to blend slightly, leaving some chunks of avocado intact.

Serve chilled with a garnish of lime wedges and whole cilantro leaves.

Blue Cheese Lorraine Miniatures

SERVES 12
(MAKES 48
MINI–CHEESE
CAKES OR
12 INDIVIDUAL
CHEESE CAKES)

These savory mini cheese cakes are perfect low-carb cocktail party bites. Make them in slightly larger (12-cup) muffin tins and serve them, individually plated, atop a luscious pile of lightly dressed mixed greens for a satisfying and delicious brunch or lunch entrée. They'll keep, tightly covered, in the refrigerator for ready-made lunches for several days.

Protein per serving:
15.5 grams

Effective carb per serving:
4.6 grams

½ pound blue cheese, room temperature
24 ounces cream cheese, softened
5 eggs
⅓ cup heavy cream
¼ teaspoon salt
¼ teaspoon freshly ground black pepper
3 to 4 dashes Tabasco sauce
1 sweet onion, finely chopped
½ pound bacon, diced small, cooked, and drained
⅓ cup almond meal
¼ cup freshly grated Parmesan cheese

Preheat the oven to 350 degrees.

Using an electric mixer or a food processor, blend together the blue cheese, cream cheese, eggs, and heavy cream until almost smooth.

Add the salt, pepper, and Tabasco and mix thoroughly.

By hand, fold in the onion and bacon.

Generously butter the cups of two mini–muffin tins (about 48 cups) or one 12-cup muffin tin.

In a separate small bowl, mix the almond meal and Parmesan cheese.

Evenly distribute this mixture into the bottoms of the buttered muffin-tin cups.

Divide the filling evenly among the cups.

Bake for about 20 minutes, turn the oven off, and leave the tins undisturbed for another 30 minutes.

Cool for 5 to 10 minutes and gently remove the cheese cakes from the tins. Serve slightly warm, or cool completely and store, tightly sealed, in the refrigerator for several days. If refrigerated, warm gently for 20 to 30 seconds in the microwave before serving.

Spicy Tortilla Triangles

SERVES 4
(8 CHIPS PER
SERVING)

Easy and quick to prepare, these tasty little bites are perfect for scooping up any low-carb dip or salsa. Their flavors remind us of the spicy pita crisps served at Trios, a favorite restaurant of ours in Little Rock, Arkansas. Try them with our Black Soybean Hummus (page 62) for a casual hors d'oeuvre with a Middle Eastern flair.

*Protein per
serving:*
5.6 grams

*Effective carb
per serving:*
3.4 grams

2 tablespoons ground cumin
2 teaspoons fine salt
1 teaspoon finely ground black pepper
¼ teaspoon cayenne pepper
4 small (taco size) low-carb tortillas
2 tablespoons olive oil (approximately)

Preheat the oven to 200 degrees.

Mix all the spices together in a ziplock bag. (If you make these chips often, you may want to triple or quadruple the spice blend recipe and keep it on hand.)

Brush one side of each tortilla with olive oil and evenly sprinkle on the spice blend.

Turn the tortillas over and repeat on the other side.

Cut the seasoned tortillas into 8 triangles, as you would a pie.

Place all the triangles in a single layer on a parchment-lined baking sheet and bake for about 20 minutes. Check them midway through, flip, and rearrange if the edges are becoming too brown.

Serve soon as the triangle chips will wilt and lose some of their appeal if left to sit at room temperature for too long.

Parmesan Crisps

MAKES 12
CRISPS

Naturally low in carb, these savory chips really dress up any salad or sit perfectly on the plate beside a bowl of soup in the place usually reserved for crackers or croutons. They're so incredibly easy to make that you can do so often. We also love to serve them as a crunchy addition to cocktail buffets or on a platter of antipasti.

Protein per serving:
3 grams

Effective carb per serving:
0.3 gram

3½ ounces Parmigiano Reggiano*
⅛ teaspoon freshly ground black pepper
⅛ teaspoon paprika
⅛ teaspoon garlic powder
pinch cayenne pepper (or to taste), optional

Preheat the oven to 300 degrees.

Finely grate the block of Parmesan cheese into a bowl.

Add all the spices and stir to distribute them evenly.

Mound the mixture by the measuring tablespoon at least 4 inches apart on a nonstick baking pad (silicon sheet) or oiled parchment on a baking sheet.

Flatten the mounds slightly and bake for about 5 minutes or until golden brown.

Cool slightly and serve. If not serving them right away, cool the crisps completely and store them in an airtight container in a cool, dry place.

*You can save grating time, if you wish, by purchasing pregrated Parmigiano Reggiano and simply using 12 tablespoons of it. Freshly grated cheese has a more intense flavor, however.

Cheesy Waffle Pizza Platforms

SERVES 6
(MAKES ABOUT
6 SEVEN-INCH
WAFFLES)

These simple waffles make the perfect thick crust for a personal pizza for kids of any age. The waffles themselves are so filling that even the hungriest adolescent may not be able to eat a whole one once it's covered with tasty pizza toppings—even if those toppings are simply Stealthy Healthy Pasta Sauce (page 238) and cheese.

Protein per serving:
17.6 grams

Effective carb per serving:
5.8 grams
(Values for protein and carb are for the waffle base only.)

1 cup almond flour
1 teaspoon baking powder
½ teaspoon salt
¼ teaspoon dried oregano
¼ cup grated Parmesan cheese
4 ounces cream cheese, softened
6 eggs
¼ cup heavy cream

Preheat a waffle iron, oiling if necessary to prevent sticking.

Mix the dry ingredients together in a small bowl.

Beat the softened cream cheese and 2 eggs until smooth. Add the remaining eggs 1 at a time and beat thoroughly between additions.

Beat in the heavy cream.

Fold in the dry ingredients. Do not overbeat at this stage or the waffles will be tough.

Spoon about ⅓ cup of batter onto the hot waffle iron and cook for about 3 minutes, until golden brown. These waffles will brown a little earlier than their high-carb cousins, so keep an eye on them.

Allow the waffles to cool slightly before adding the pizza toppings. The waffles will also freeze well for later use. Simply cool completely, separate them with paper towels, enclose in ziplock freezer bags, and store in the freezer for several weeks.

Country Corn Bread

SERVES 12

Those growing up in a Southern home come to expect a skillet of hot corn bread with certain meals. It was always served, for instance, split and covered with black-eyed peas on New Year's Day. (Yes, the peas are high in carb, but they bring good luck; it's just one day a year, so enjoy!) Sometimes, corn bread appeared as a light meal, crumbled into a tall glass of milk or buttermilk and eaten with a spoon. It's best made in a well-seasoned cast-iron skillet with hot bacon drippings—just like Mom used to do it—but however you make it, this version will please your palate without breaking your carb budget.

Protein per serving:
8.2 grams

Effective carb per serving:
7.6 grams

½ cup cornmeal
1½ cups almond flour
¼ cup wheat bran
1 teaspoon salt
1½ teaspoons baking powder
2 eggs
¾ cup half-and-half
¾ cup water

Preheat the oven to 375 degrees.

Melt about 2 tablespoons of bacon drippings or butter in an 8-inch cast-iron skillet (or an 8-inch cake pan).

Meanwhile, in a bowl, combine all the dry ingredients.

In a separate bowl, beat together the eggs, half-and-half, and water.

Stir the liquid ingredients into the dry ingredients and thoroughly combine.

Pour the batter into the preheated fat in the hot skillet and bake for 25 to 30 minutes until the edges are slightly brown and pulling away from the pan. A toothpick inserted into the center should come out clean.

Serve immediately, if possible, with unsalted butter.

Cornmeal Johnnycakes

MAKES 8 CAKES

Something akin to savory pancakes and a little like blinis, these little corn cakes are not only delicious, but they pack some protein, too. They're just perfect alongside a big steaming bowl of chili, stew, or soup, and so easy you'll want to stir up a batch often.

Protein per serving:
13.3 grams

Effective carb per serving:
6.2 grams

¾ cup almond flour
¼ cup yellow cornmeal, coarsely ground
¼ cup natural flavor, low-carb whey protein powder
¾ teaspoon baking powder
¼ teaspoon salt
¼ teaspoon ground cumin
⅛ teaspoon garlic powder
⅛ teaspoon cayenne pepper
2 eggs
¾ cup half-and-half
1 tablespoon unsalted butter

Heat a griddle or a large skillet over medium heat.

Mix all the dry ingredients, including the salt and spices, in a small mixing bowl.

In a separate bowl, beat together the eggs and the half-and-half.

Stir the dry ingredients into the wet ones to make a batter.

Melt the butter on the griddle just before use.

Pour a scant ¼ cup of the batter onto the griddle for each cake, leaving a little room between them, and cook for a couple of minutes. When they are golden on the first side, flip and cook a minute or two on the other.

Serve immediately.

Garlic Parmesan Griddle Bread

A bit like a savory French toast, these bread sticks pack more protein punch than regular garlic toast, and they're perfect for sopping up marinara sauce or broth. Kids and parents alike will love them to dip into a bowl of Double Red Soup (page 240).

Protein per serving:
7.3 grams

Effective carb per serving:
7.7 grams

4 slices commercial low-carb bread
1 egg, beaten
½ cup half-and-half
1 teaspoon garlic powder
¼ teaspoon salt
1 teaspoon chopped fresh rosemary or ½ teaspoon dried
1 tablespoon freshly grated Parmesan cheese
1 tablespoon unsalted butter

Trim the crust from the bread slices* and cut each slice lengthwise into 2 or 3 long rectangles.

In a shallow bowl, combine all the remaining ingredients, except the butter.

On the stove, heat a griddle or a large skillet over medium heat. Melt the butter until it foams.

Dip both sides of each rectangle of bread in the egg mixture and fry until golden brown on the first side, 2 to 3 minutes; flip and brown the other side.

Serve immediately or hold in a single layer on a baking sheet, uncovered, in a warm oven for up to 20 minutes.

*Make bread crumbs of the saved crusts by pulsing them in a food processor. Store them in ziplock freezer bags until you're ready to use them.

Handmade Rye Bread*

**MAKES 24
SERVINGS
(4 LOAVES)**

A warm chunk of crusty bread can make the simplest soup a meal. Even if you don't consider yourself a baker, you'll be surprised at how easily you can turn out these tasty loaves. Make a double or even triple batch, because the loaves freeze well. Just thaw them in the refrigerator and reheat them gently in the oven.

*Protein per
serving:*
4.7 grams

*Effective carb
per serving:*
4.3 grams

¾ cup hot water
1 cup cold water
2 tablespoons olive oil
1 package rapid-rise yeast
1¼ cups almond flour
1¼ cups wheat bran
1 cup vital wheat gluten
2 tablespoons ThickenThin not/Sugar (see page 9)
⅔ cup dark rye flour
¾ teaspoon salt

Preheat the oven to 200 degrees.

Lightly grease a nonstick baking sheet with olive oil.

In a large mixing bowl, combine the hot and cold water and the olive oil. Stir in the yeast and allow to activate—you will see small bubbles forming in the mixture after about 5 minutes.

In a separate bowl, mix the dry ingredients together, and once the yeast mixture has activated, add the dry ingredients to the wet ones and bring together with a fork.

Lightly oil your palms and take over by hand, kneading the bread dough for 5 minutes. Use a bit more oil if needed to keep the dough from being sticky.

Turn off the oven.

Divide the dough into quarters and shape each quarter into a round or a log-shaped baguette.

Place the dough onto an oiled baking sheet in the oven and allow the dough to rise for an hour or so until it has tripled in size.

Leaving the bread in the oven, turn it on to 350 degrees and bake for about 30 minutes.

Cool and slice the round loaves into 6 wedges, the baguettes into 6 thick slices.

*Adapted from The
Low-Carb Comfort
Food Cookbook.*

Rosemary and Olive Pan Bread

SERVES 9

Reminiscent of focaccia and of onion loaf, this savory bread makes a wonderful accompaniment to meat and poultry dishes as well as hearty soups. It's so filling, it even makes a substantial appetizer with wine and antipasti before going to the theater or a concert. If you multiply the recipe for a bigger gathering, make it in two or more 9-inch pans to ensure even baking.

Protein per serving:
13.5 grams

Effective carb per serving:
10.4 grams

2 tablespoons plus 1 tablespoon unsalted butter (divided for use)
1 medium onion, thinly sliced
1 cup sliced black or kalamata olives
1 tablespoon fresh rosemary leaves
1 teaspoon finely minced fresh rosemary
¼ teaspoon salt
¼ teaspoon freshly ground black pepper
1 cup almond flour
½ cup whole-wheat flour
¼ cup wheat bran
¼ cup low-carb, natural flavor whey protein powder
1 tablespoon baking powder
1 egg
½ cup half-and-half
½ cup water
¼ cup light olive oil

Preheat the oven to 350 degrees.

Butter a 9-inch-square cake pan with 1 tablespoon of butter.

In a skillet, melt the remaining butter over medium heat. When it's foamy, add the onions and sauté for 8 to 10 minutes until they soften; stir occasionally. Add the olives and whole rosemary leaves and stir briefly to combine.

Turn the onion mixture into the bottom of the cake pan.

In a bowl, combine all of the dry ingredients, including the minced rosemary.

In a separate bowl, beat the egg, half-and-half, water, and olive oil.

Add the egg mixture to the dry ingredients and stir together just to combine.

Spread this batter over the olive and onion mixture in the cake pan and bake for about 35 minutes until a toothpick inserted into the center comes out clean.

Let the bread stand for a few minutes, invert it onto a serving plate, cut into 9 squares, and serve warm.

CHAPTER 4

◇   ◇   ◇

Soups, Salads, and Dressings

◇   ◇   ◇

◇   ◇   ◇

We're big soup fans. When we're tired or rushed and we just want something light but filling for dinner, we'll stir up a big pot of chicken vegetable soup, using up whatever vegetables we might have on hand; we toss a salad, pour a glass of wine, and relax. Soup's the hands-down winner among budget-friendly foods—it will stretch easily to feed unexpected guests, and whatever's left becomes a ready-made lunch for the next day.

What you may not realize, however, is that soup can be an ally in your weight-control efforts; it's sort of like an automatic calorie reduction system. Served as a first course for a meal, soup helps to quell your hunger, fills you up somewhat, and allows you to eat less of the main course and enjoy it all the more. A soup course is a way to bring interesting color and texture to a meal, as well as a way to painlessly increase your family's intake of antioxidant-rich vegetables that they may not commonly enjoy. When veggies are served as soups, picky eaters won't think of them as vegetables. For instance, give our Cream of Asparagus Soup or our Beet and Ginger Soup a whirl; even if you've never been a big fan of asparagus or beets, we think you'll be pleasantly surprised.

And on a chilly day in the fall or the winter, what could be more enjoyable than ladling up a big steaming bowl of hearty soup, chowder, or chili? (The latter, since it's full of meaty goodness, you'll find in chapter 5.) These soups have enough heft to satisfy even the biggest appetites; simply pair them with one of the savory breads you'll find in chapter 3 and a bottle of low-carb beer or a glass of vino, if you're so inclined. If you love soup as a meal unto itself, then you're sure to enjoy a creamy bowl of our Roasted Butternut Squash Soup, Black Soybean Soup, or our New England–Style Clam Chowder, where we've used diced celery root (a fantastic potato imposter) in place of the potatoes with scarcely a hint of difference.

Celery root, a vegetable you may not be familiar with, is precisely what it says it is: the root from which springs the more familiar green stalks of celery. In the market, you'll usually find the root itself, sort of a gnarly brown blob about the size of a softball, somewhere in the fresh produce section by the beets, turnips, jicama, parsnips, and other root veggies. If it's not at your store, ask your produce manager; it can be ordered from the supplier for you. Select one that's dense and moist— if it seems too light for its size, it's probably old and dried out and won't be tender when cooked. Once you get it home, rinse if off—it should look like it was just pulled out of the ground a few minutes ago. Cut off the ends, the wider bottom, and the top with remnants of celery stalk stumps with a sharp chef's knife, then peel the outer brown skin away just as you would a potato. Celery root is a nutritional bargain, having cup for cup all the useful nutrients but only about a third of the carbohydrates and about half the calories of potato.

What's soup without salad? Greens are always a low-carb bargain, with a lot of nutritional bang for the carb buck, particularly if you select a variety of colorful low-starch veggies—peppers, squash, beets, carrots, broccoli, cauliflower, mushrooms, tomatoes, asparagus, sprouts—to mix with them. Those kinds of salads are fairly self-evidently low-carb foods and don't require a lot of explanation. You can toss them up as you like and top them with good-quality olive oil vinaigrettes anytime. What we've tried to include here are some of our old favorites, such as Creamy Southern Coleslaw and Guacamole Salad, and the classic picnic standby, potato salad, reincarnated in low-carb form as Fauxtato Salad, once again through the magic of celery root. Along with these classics, we've included some slightly more unusual preparations, such as the Classic Wedge Salad, our Creamy Crunchy Veggie Salad, and a Fresh Zucchini Salad that we think you will enjoy. Who says low-carb means no veggies?

Black Soybean Soup

SERVES 4

The Caribbean flavors of this hearty soup make us think longingly of after-dinner strolls along the sugar sand, moonlight on the waves, and a gentle breeze blowing in from the water, an especially nice thought when the weather turns chill. Then, a warming soup is just the ticket. Made with the vegetable stock option, it's a great meal for low-carbing vegetarians.

Protein per serving:
15.7 grams

Effective carb per serving:
13.1 grams

2 tablespoons coconut oil
1 carrot, finely chopped
1 medium onion, chopped
2 cloves garlic, minced
1 tablespoon chili powder
1 quart chicken or vegetable stock
1 teaspoon salt
1½ teaspoons freshly ground black pepper
2 cans (about 3 cups) black soybeans, rinsed and drained
2 tablespoons ThickenThin not/Starch (see page 9), optional*

GARNISH
1 lime, quartered
1 tablespoon Mexican Cream (page 171)
1 green onion, chopped

In a large saucepan, melt the coconut oil over medium heat.

Add the carrot and onion and sauté until soft, about 5 minutes.

Add the garlic and chili powder and sauté another minute or two.

Add the stock, salt, and pepper and bring to a boil (see the option in the footnote).

Add the black soybeans, reduce the heat to low, and allow to simmer for 10 minutes.

With a potato masher, mash some of the beans to thicken the broth slightly.

When ready to serve, garnish each bowl with a lime quarter, a squiggle of Mexican Cream, and a sprinkling of chopped green onion. Squeeze the lime wedge over the soup.

*For a thicker broth, whisk in the ThickenThin before adding the soybeans.

New England–Style Clam Chowder

SERVES 4

What could be more warming on a chilly day than a steaming cup of creamy clam chowder? But most versions of this New England classic come laden with more potatoes than clams, and some are thickened with flour roux. We've sidestepped those carby ingredients by filling ours with diced celery root and thickening it with fiber thickeners but retained all the creaminess and clamminess that make us love it in any season.

Protein per serving:
22 grams

Effective carb per serving:
13 grams

1 cup celery root, peeled and diced
1 teaspoon salt plus additional, if desired
4 to 6 slices bacon, minced
1 cup peeled and minced onion
½ cup diced celery
2 cups chicken stock
1 teaspoon ground white pepper
1 teaspoon fresh thyme or ½ teaspoon dried
2 tablespoons ThickenThin not/Starch (see page 9)
2 cups half-and-half
2 cups shucked clams
1 tablespoon unsalted butter

In a medium saucepan, cover the celery root with water, add the salt, and bring to a boil. Boil for 10 to 15 minutes, until soft enough to pierce easily with the tip of a knife.

Meanwhile, fry the bacon pieces until crisp. Remove the bacon with a slotted spoon and reserve.

In the bacon grease that remains, over medium heat, cook the onion and celery until limp.

Add the cooked celery root and chicken stock, pepper, and thyme. Bring the mixture to a boil. (At this point, you can stop, cool the chowder broth, and hold it in an airtight container in the refrigerator for a day or two before proceeding. When ready to serve, bring the broth to a boil, reduce the heat, and continue with the next step.) Taste for salt, as the saltiness of the bacon drippings may be sufficient. Add salt, if desired.

Reduce the heat to low. Add ThickenThin to the soup, stirring with a whisk until the broth begins to thicken somewhat. If thicker chowder is desired, whisk in another 1 to 2 teaspoons of thickener.

Stir in the half-and-half and the clams.

Add the butter and allow it to just melt.

Garnish with a teaspoon of reserved bacon bits. Serve immediately.

Roasted Red Pepper Soup*

SERVES 4

Colorful, flavorful, and full of vitamins, minerals, and antioxidants, this beautiful soup is delicious chilled or hot. It's elegant enough to start a formal dinner and easy enough to serve with a low-carb grilled cheese sandwich for lunch anytime.

Protein per serving:
1.6 grams

Effective carb per serving:
2.6 grams

2 jars roasted red peppers (1½ to 2 cups)
1 can (15 ounces) chicken broth
1 clove garlic, pressed or minced
½ teaspoon coarse salt
¼ teaspoon freshly ground black pepper
⅛ teaspoon cayenne pepper

GARNISH
1 tablespoon finely minced fresh cilantro
1 tablespoon sour cream
1 tablespoon half-and-half

Drain and rinse the peppers, removing any remaining pith or seeds.

Place the peppers, chicken broth, garlic, and spices into a blender and puree until smooth.

Chill the soup for at least one hour.

When ready to serve, in a small bowl, whisk the cilantro with the sour cream and half-and-half and garnish each bowl with a drizzled flourish of the mixture.

*Adapted from Chilled Red Pepper Soup with Cilantro in *Protein Power*.

French Onion Soup

SERVES 6

Hearty, savory, and filling, this lower-carb take on the beloved classic starter retains all the stringy cheesy enjoyment of the original. It makes a great beginning to dinner, stands alone quite nicely, or is excellent when paired with a salad or a wrap for lunch.

Protein per serving:
16.8 grams

Effective carb per serving:
8.7 grams

3 tablespoons unsalted butter
3 medium yellow onions, thinly sliced
1 cup dry white wine*
6 cups beef broth
1 bouquet garni (3 to 4 stems parsley, 1 bay leaf, 1 sprig thyme, tied)
1 teaspoon salt
1 teaspoon freshly ground black pepper
6 slices commercial low-carb bread
1½ cups grated Gruyère cheese

In a large saucepan, melt the butter over medium-high heat until it foams; add the onions and sauté briefly. When the onions give up their moisture, reduce the heat to medium and continue to cook, stirring occasionally, until they reach a dark golden brown. Do not allow them to burn.

Add the wine and continue to cook the onions until the wine evaporates completely.

Add the beef broth and bring slowly to a boil; add the bouquet garni, salt, and pepper. Reduce to a simmer and continue to cook until the total volume of soup is reduced to approximately 5 cups, about 45 minutes.

Meanwhile, preheat the oven to 200 degrees.

Trim the slices of bread to fit your soup bowl and toast them in the oven until dry.†

Ladle the soup equally into 6 ovenproof soup bowls. Place the bowls onto a baking sheet.

Top each bowl with a slice of toasted bread and ¼ cup of the grated cheese.

Slip them under the broiler for about 2 minutes to melt the cheese.

Serve immediately.

*If you prefer not to use wine, substitute an additional 1 cup of beef broth or water.

†Make bread crumbs of the saved crusts by pulsing them in a food processor. Store them in ziplock freezer bags until you're ready to use them.

Cream of Asparagus Soup

SERVES 4

In our house, asparagus is a staple food. We love it roasted, steamed, stir-fried, in salads, and made into soup. Besides being a real low-carb star, it's chockful of healthful micronutrients and natural cancer-fighters. This presentation is both elegant enough to entertain with and easy enough to make often.

Protein per serving:
5.4 grams

Effective carb per serving:
7 grams

12 to 15 fresh asparagus spears, washed and trimmed
2 tablespoons unsalted butter
1 small shallot, peeled and minced
½ teaspoon salt (divided for use)
½ teaspoon white pepper (divided for use)
3 cups vegetable broth
2 tablespoons ThickenThin not/Starch (see page 9)
1 cup half-and-half (at room temperature)
1 tablespoon chopped fresh flat-leaf parsley
4 tablespoons crème fraîche

Chop the asparagus spears into 2-inch lengths, preserving the tips for the garnish.

Place the pieces into a microwave-safe dish, add 1 tablespoon of water, cover, and microwave on high for about 3 minutes to soften them.

Melt the butter in a 2-quart saucepan over medium heat until it foams. Add the shallot and sauté until translucent. Add the asparagus pieces, season with a pinch of the salt and white pepper, and sauté for a minute or two.

Transfer the asparagus and shallots to a blender or a food processor. Add the vegetable broth, ThickenThin, and remaining salt and pepper and puree until smooth. At this point, the soup can be held, covered and refrigerated, for up to a day before proceeding.

Return the soup to the saucepan, bring it to a boil, reduce the heat to simmer, and stir in the half-and-half. Just before serving, stir in the parsley.

Ladle the soup into bowls; place a dollop of crème fraîche and ¼ of the reserved asparagus tips in the center of each bowl.

Beet and Ginger Soup

SERVES 4

Although we think of this soup in the spring, the earthiness of the beets and the bright flavors of ginger, lemon, and cilantro make it irresistible any season of the year. And don't forget that the bright colors—deep red, bright yellow, and green—mean that some wonderfully healthful antioxidant or phytochemical resides within.

Protein per serving:
3.5 grams

Effective carb per serving:
10.2 grams

4 medium beets
2½ tablespoons grated or minced fresh ginger
4 cups vegetable broth
4 tablespoons fresh lemon juice, plus the zest of 1 lemon
1 teaspoon salt
½ teaspoon freshly ground black pepper
4 small cilantro sprigs (for garnish)

Thoroughly wash and trim the beets; place them into a saucepan, cover with water, and cover the pan. Bring to a boil, reduce the heat, and simmer for 1 hour.

When cool enough to handle, under running water, slip off the beet skins. They should come off easily. (You can cook and peel the beets ahead of time and hold them in a ziplock bag or an airtight container in the refrigerator for up to a day or two.)

Coarsely chop the beets and put them into a blender or a food processor.

Add the ginger, vegetable broth, lemon juice, salt, and pepper and puree until smooth.

If desired, return the soup to the saucepan to warm thoroughly or chill for an hour in the refrigerator and serve cold.

When ready to serve, ladle the soup into bowls and garnish each with a sprig of cilantro and a sprinkling of lemon zest.

Roasted Butternut Squash Soup

SERVES 6

Hearty, filling, and delicious, this is one of our all-time favorite soups and one that we make often for family and friends. While it's certainly not ultra-low-carb, it packs a good nutritional bang—especially in beta-carotene and potassium—for the carb buck.

Protein per serving:
2.4 grams

Effective carb per serving:
14 grams

1 butternut squash (about 10 inches long)
6 tablespoons unsalted butter (divided for use)
½ teaspoon salt (plus a pinch, to taste)
¼ teaspoon freshly ground black pepper (plus a pinch, to taste)
¼ teaspoon ground cinnamon
⅛ teaspoon freshly ground nutmeg
½ medium yellow onion, peeled and diced
1 small tart green apple, peeled and diced
3 cups vegetable broth or water

Preheat the oven to 400 degrees.

Remove the stem end from the butternut squash and split the squash in half lengthwise. Scoop out and discard the seeds.

Dot the squash halves with 1 tablespoon of butter and sprinkle on the salt, pepper, cinnamon, and nutmeg.

Roast the squash for 45 minutes to 1 hour until fork tender.

Meanwhile, melt another tablespoon of butter in a 2-quart saucepan over medium heat; when the butter foams, add the onion and apple, season lightly with salt and pepper, and sauté until tender. Set aside.

When the squash is cool enough to handle, use a large spoon to scoop the pulp into a blender or a food processor. Add the sautéed onion and apple and about half of the vegetable broth and process until smooth. Return the soup to the saucepan, add the remaining liquid to the desired thickness, and keep warm over low heat. At this point, the soup can be cooked and refrigerated in a covered container and held for 24 hours. Return the soup to a saucepan and bring it to a simmer before proceeding.

In a small skillet over medium heat, melt the remaining butter and cook it until it is a deep golden brown.

Ladle the soup into bowls, drizzle some of the browned butter into each one, and serve immediately.

Mixed Fruit Salad

SERVES 8

The criticism that a low-carb diet contains no fruit or vegetables is, of course, false. We encourage consumption of a wide variety of low-sugar, high-fiber choices, such as berries and melons—the variety is almost endless. This recipe uses cantaloupe, strawberries, and kiwi, but try honeydew, blackberries, and raspberries for a change. These tasty and colorful combinations look gorgeous on the plate and pack plenty of vitamins, antioxidants, and phytochemicals for good health with a small carb expenditure.

Protein per serving:
0.6 gram

Effective carb per serving:
6.5 grams

½ cantaloupe, peeled, seeded, and cut into small chunks
2 cups fresh stemmed and quartered strawberries
1 kiwi, peeled and diced
1 lime, juice and zest
1 tablespoon granular Splenda
fresh mint (for garnish)

Combine all the fruits in a large bowl.

Add the lime juice, lime zest, and Splenda and stir to coat all the fruit.

Garnish with a fresh mint sprig, if desired.

Guacamole Salad

Whether you serve this as a dip with low-carb chips or as a salad course with any south of the border meal, you can't beat the bright flavors and nutritional bang of fresh, homemade guacamole. This recipe calls for just one Serrano pepper, but if you really like it hot, crank it up with more peppers or leave in a few of the seeds, which is where much of the heat resides.

Protein per serving:
2.9 grams

Effective carb per serving:
5 grams

1 small red onion, diced small
1 lime, juiced
1 clove garlic, minced
2 ripe Haas avocados
2 Roma (or small red) tomatoes, seeded and diced small
½ teaspoon salt (or to taste)
½ teaspoon freshly ground black pepper (or to taste)
1 Serrano pepper, seeded and minced
1 handful fresh cilantro, chopped
2 to 3 cups fresh romaine lettuce, cut julienne-style

In a small bowl, soak the diced onion in just enough water to cover it and 1 tablespoon of lime juice for 5 to 10 minutes to take the bite out of the raw onion. Drain the bowl before using the onion.

In a separate glass or nonmetal bowl, combine the remaining lime juice and the minced garlic.

Peel and seed the avocados, dice, put into the bowl with the lime juice and garlic, and mash until smooth.

Add the tomatoes, the onions, salt, pepper, minced Serrano pepper, and cilantro and mix to combine.

Taste for seasoning; add more spices as desired.

Serve the salad on a bed of romaine lettuce.

If not to be eaten immediately, cover by placing a sheet of plastic wrap directly onto the surface of the guacamole to seal out all air. Cover the bowl with another piece of plastic and refrigerate. Bring the guacamole to room temperature before serving.

Fauxtato Salad

SERVES 4 TO 6

For a barbecue feast, nothing sits quite as handsomely on the plate beside the ham, chicken, brisket, or ribs as a serving of potato salad. For those following a low-carb diet, however, the serving winds up being pretty meager. Not so with this mock version, which relies on celery root instead of potatoes as the base. This has all the flavor and mouthfeel of the original, with a fraction of the carbs.

Protein per serving:
4.5 grams

Effective carb per serving:
7 grams

2 cups celery root, peeled and diced small
1 teaspoon plus ¼ teaspoon salt (divided for use)
2 tablespoons cider vinegar or white wine vinegar (divided in half for use)
¼ small red onion, peeled and diced
1 can (14 ounces) sliced black olives
1 rib celery, diced small
½ cup minced fresh flat-leaf parsley
2 hard-boiled eggs, peeled and chopped
½ cup Basic Blender Mayonnaise (page 169)
1 teaspoon Dijon mustard
¼ teaspoon garlic powder
¼ teaspoon freshly ground black pepper
¼ teaspoon paprika

In a medium saucepan, cover the diced celery root with water, add 1 teaspoon of salt, cover, and bring to a boil. Continue boiling for about 15 minutes until it is fork tender. Drain well.

Meanwhile, soak the onion for 10 to 15 minutes in a cup of water and 1 tablespoon of vinegar. Drain well.

In a large bowl, combine the celery root, onion, olives, celery, parsley, and egg.

In a separate small bowl, make a dressing by whisking together the mayonnaise, mustard, spices (including the remaining salt), and the remaining vinegar. Add this mixture to the vegetables and toss to coat evenly.

Cover the Fauxtato Salad and refrigerate it if not serving it right away.

Creamy Southern Coleslaw

SERVES 8

This creamy, crunchy Southern favorite is a required dish for any down-home barbecue, picnic, or fish fry, but it sits nicely on the plate with crab cakes or low-carb tortilla wraps, too. The taste is the same, but the sugar and bad fats have been changed to protect the innocent—us!

Protein per serving:
0.6 gram

Effective carb per serving:
2.5 grams

½ cup Basic Blender Mayonnaise (page 169)
2 tablespoons cider vinegar or white wine vinegar
½ teaspoon celery seed
½ teaspoon salt
½ teaspoon freshly ground black pepper
1 to 2 packets Splenda
3 cups shredded red or green cabbage*
1 red bell pepper, seeded and finely chopped
1 small carrot, peeled and grated

In a large salad bowl, whisk together the mayonnaise, vinegar, spices, and Splenda.

Add the cabbage, bell pepper, and carrot and toss to coat evenly. Cover and refrigerate for several hours, if possible, before serving. Keep cool if transporting to serve alfresco.

*As a time-saver, use 3½ cups of a prepackaged slaw mix in place of the cabbage, bell pepper, and carrot.

Creamy Crunchy Veggie Salad

SERVES 4

You can make this colorful, nutritious salad in a matter of minutes, and, unlike leafy green salads, it will keep for several days in the refrigerator. It's one of our favorite ways to enjoy the crisp crunch of fresh vegetables with any meal. Make a double recipe to have plenty of leftovers for lunch the next day or two.

Protein per serving:
5.3 grams

Effective carb per serving:
6.2 grams

1 cup broccoli florets
1 cup cauliflower florets
1 cup sliced radishes
1 yellow bell pepper, seeded and diced
2 tablespoons white wine vinegar
½ teaspoon coarse salt
½ teaspoon freshly ground black pepper
¼ teaspoon garlic powder
¼ teaspoon paprika
½ cup cream
¼ cup grated Parmesan cheese

Wash and trim all vegetables; cut any large florets into smaller pieces. Blanche briefly (30 seconds) in boiling water, if desired, although it's not necessary. Dry the vegetables thoroughly.

In a mixing bowl, combine the vinegar, salt, pepper, and spices. Whisk in the cream and then add the Parmesan cheese, stirring to combine.

Add the vegetables and toss to coat completely. Serve.

Store any leftovers in a tightly sealed container in the refrigerator.

Fresh Zucchini Salad

Zucchini is one of the low-carb stars among vegetables. We love it grilled, roasted, sautéed, in soups, and, yes, even raw in salads. Here it is the salad. We're sure you'll love this easy presentation: the crisp bite and mild flavor of the zucchini set off by the salty tang of the Parmigiano. This dish is not the place to scrimp on the quality of olive oil; select an extra-virgin pressing of your favorite variety— Greek, Spanish, Italian, Californian—and let its vibrant, full-bodied, green flavor shine.

Protein per serving:
4.3 grams

Effective carb per serving:
3 grams

4 small zucchini
1 tablespoon white wine vinegar
½ teaspoon coarse salt
¼ teaspoon freshly ground black pepper
½ teaspoon freshly minced basil leaves
2 tablespoons olive oil
1 ounce (approximately) Parmigiano Reggiano

Wash, pat dry, stem, and slice the zucchini into thin rounds.

In a small bowl, combine the vinegar, salt, pepper, and basil and allow it to sit for a few minutes. Whisk in the oil to make the vinaigrette.

Pour the vinaigrette over the zucchini rounds and toss to coat evenly.

Divide the dressed zucchini evenly among four plates, shave Parmesan curls generously over each plate, and serve.

Mixed Greens with Spicy Lime Vinaigrette

SERVES 4

Leafy greens, not only low in carb but packed with fiber, folate, and other vitamins, are a low carber's best friend. Although this recipe specifies enough greens for a side salad with dinner—about a cup— feel free to pile on all the mixed lettuces, fresh spinach, endive, radicchio, or arugula you want. Remember to dress it lightly, because although it's very low in carb, there are plenty of calories in the olive oil dressing.

Protein per serving:
1 gram

Effective carb per serving:
1.4 grams

1 small garlic clove
½ teaspoon coarse salt
1 lime, juiced
½ teaspoon freshly ground black pepper
¼ teaspoon cumin
⅛ teaspoon cayenne pepper
1 packet Splenda
3 tablespoons extra-virgin olive oil
4 cups fresh mixed greens, washed and dried

Finely mince the garlic on a cutting board and top with the coarse salt. Lay the blade of a chef's knife flat across the minced garlic, press down, and repeatedly draw the edge of the blade across the garlic in a stroking motion to crush the garlic and salt into a slightly chunky paste.

Place the garlic paste into a small bowl, add the lime juice, pepper, spices, and Splenda and combine. Set aside for at least 5 minutes to marry the flavors.

Just before serving, whisk in the olive oil to make a smooth emulsion.

Pour the dressing over the greens, toss to coat lightly and evenly, and serve.

Blue Cheese Dressing

SERVES 8

Hands down, this is our favorite creamy dressing, and if you're a fan of the tangy sharpness of blue cheese, this recipe is sure to please you, too. Those of us who love stinky cheeses will enjoy using the stronger blues, such as Stilton or Roquefort. Others who don't appreciate pungent, tangy cheeses might prefer to use a milder blue, such as Gorgonzola Dolce or Creamy Danish Blue.

Protein per serving:
3.7 grams

Effective carb per serving:
1.2 grams

4 ounces blue cheese (divided in half for use)
½ cup Basic Blender Mayonnaise (page 169)
¼ cup crème fraîche or sour cream
¼ cup half-and-half
1 teaspoon Dijon mustard
2 teaspoons soy sauce
2 tablespoons fresh lemon juice
¼ teaspoon salt
¼ teaspoon freshly ground black pepper

Place half of the blue cheese and all the remaining ingredients into a blender or a food processor and blend until smooth.

Add the remaining blue cheese and pulse a time or two, aiming to leave lumps of blue cheese visible in the dressing.

Pour the dressing into a container with a tight-fitting lid and store in the refrigerator for up to one week.

Classic Wedge Salad

SERVES 4

One of our very favorite salads, served at great steakhouses from New York to Chicago to Santa Barbara, is a very simple one: the wedge. We once ordered one at Angelo and Maxie's in Manhattan that was so huge it could have been dinner for a family of four; it must have come from a head of iceberg lettuce the size of a basketball. When we make ours at home, we try to select a slightly smaller head, unless our wedge is to be dinner all by itself.

Protein per serving:
10.3 grams

Effective carb per serving:
4.9 grams

1 medium-size head iceberg lettuce
½ recipe Blue Cheese Dressing (page 95)
1 ripe Roma (or small red) tomato, seeded and diced
2 ounces blue cheese, crumbled
4 slices cooked bacon, crumbled

Wash the lettuce and remove any ragged outer leaves. Cut the head into quarters.

Place one quarter onto each serving plate, top each with 2 to 3 tablespoons of the Blue Cheese Dressing, then sprinkle on ¼ of the diced tomato, ¼ of the blue cheese crumbles, and ¼ of the crumbled bacon.

Serve immediately.

CHAPTER 5

◇　◇　◇

Meat, Poultry, Fish, and Shellfish

Dry-Rubbed, Slow-Roasted Baby Back Ribs

Medallions of Beef Tenderloin with Cabernet Reduction

Shepherd's Pie

Luscious Lasagna

Red Chile Rolled Enchiladas

Three-Alarm Chili

White Chili

Spicy Southern Fried Chicken

Barbecued Chicken Hot Wings

Oven-Barbecued Hot Wings

Green Chile Chicken Enchiladas

Chicken Potpie

Chicken Satay

Chicken Mushroom Packets

Thai Red Chile Chicken

Fish and Pepper Packets

Tilapia Soft Tacos

Seafood Casserole

Crab Cakes

A-Lot-Like-Lacquered Salmon

Shrimp Quesadilla

◇　　◇　　◇

◇　◇　◇

Clearly, meat, poultry, fish, and shellfish are the main food categories that are at the heart of a protein-rich diet; there's no great secret that they are, in fact, low carb, and in most cases it takes no great magic to make them so. After all, beef tenderloin is dandy just the way it is; barbecued chicken wings need no special alchemy to make them deliciously low in carb, just plenty of chile to set your taste buds aflame. This chapter will offer a few surprises, though, in our adaptations of some higher-carb entrées, such as Shepherd's Pie topped with Creamed Fauxtatoes made from celery root in place of mashed potatoes and Chicken Potpie that bubbles with silken goodness beneath our low-carb Tender Almond Pie and Tart Crust.

You'll find some traditionally high-carb ethnic favorites here, too, such as the Luscious Lasagna, layered with fresh lasagna noodles made from our Impasta Almond Flour Pasta Dough, much lower in carb, much higher in protein, and completely deelish. Here, as well, you'll find two takes on enchiladas: the first, Red Chile Rolled Enchiladas, made with ground ostrich, and the second, Green Chile Chicken Enchiladas, made in layers the traditional Northern New Mexican way. Both owe their carb reduction to the advent of good commercially available low-carb tortillas. Even Asian food fans can fill their bowls with low-carb flavor, enjoying the Chicken Satay and the Thai Red Chile Chicken, served not over rice or noodles but rather over our Spagaroni, made from spaghetti squash.

And for the seafood lover in you, we've got delicious Crab Cakes (made with low-carb bread crumbs) and one of our all-time favorite recipes, A-Lot-Like-Lacquered Salmon, a sweet, peppery hot, and fragrant delight.

We've tried to make all the entrées, whether meat, poultry, or seafood, easy to prepare; some of the recipes, such as Fish and Pepper Packets and Chicken Mushroom Packets, cook right in their own foil packs and don't even require cleanup. Fish and chicken lend themselves to this preparation, but thinly sliced pork chops, thin pork or beef medallions, slices of kielbasa, shrimp, scallops, or even hamburger patties will work, too. Kids love the novelty of packet meals, and moms and dads will appreciate the time and energy savings of these easy-to-do hobo dinner specials. Just because protein should be the cornerstone of the meal doesn't mean it has to be difficult or time-consuming.

Dry-Rubbed, Slow-Roasted Baby Back Ribs

**SERVES 4
(OR 2 VERY BIG
APPETITES)**

There's nothing we love better than a rib feast. We prefer the dry-rubbed version with the sauce on the side that recalls our many trips to what we consider the mecca of the rib world, The Rendezvous in Memphis, Tennessee. Cook them low and slow for that falling-off-the-bone tenderness we equate with ribs done right.

*Protein per
serving (for 4):*
36.6 grams

*Effective carb
per serving (for 4):*
2.8 grams

BABY BACK RIB RUB
2 racks of baby back ribs
4 tablespoons Lower-Carb Dry Rub for Meats (page 167)

BASTING SOLUTION
2 cups water
½ cup vinegar
2 tablespoons olive oil
1 tablespoon chili powder
cayenne pepper to taste

Very lightly oil the ribs with olive oil.

Sprinkle the Dry Rub for Meats (about 1 tablespoon per side) onto the ribs.

Wrap the seasoned racks of ribs in plastic wrap and refrigerate for at least 1 hour; bring the ribs to room temperature before cooking.

Preheat the oven to 275 to 300 degrees or set a grill fire to medium-low heat.

TO COOK IN THE OVEN

Place a wire cooling rack onto a baking sheet, and to make cleanup easier, line the baking sheet with foil and liberally grease the wire rack.

Remove the plastic wrap from the ribs.

Place the rib racks on the wire rack onto the baking sheet.

Roast the meat for about 1½ hours, until quite tender. The meat should easily pull away from the bone.

TO COOK ON THE GRILL

Whether gas or charcoal, the grill heat should be medium-low (275 to 300 degrees).

Cover the center of the grill grate with a sheet of aluminum foil to prevent flare-ups, but leave a margin around the foil for heat to circulate freely.

Arrange the ribs on oiled rib racks, if you have them, or place the ribs directly on the foil on the grill grate and close the cover of the grill.

Roast in the closed grill for 1½ to 2 hours, until the meat easily pulls away from the bone.

While the ribs are cooking, make the basting solution. In a saucepan, combine the water, vinegar, olive oil, chili powder, and cayenne pepper and bring to a quick boil. Set the mixture aside to cool.

Directly out of the oven or hot off the grill, douse or "mop" the hot racks with the basting solution, wrap in foil, further wrap with several thicknesses of newspaper, and allow the meat to rest for 15 to 20 minutes.

Serve with Spicy Mustard BBQ Sauce (page 168) or a low-carb commercial barbecue sauce on the side, if desired.

Medallions of Beef Tenderloin with Cabernet Reduction

Easy and elegant, this most impressive dish will make you a culinary star. Our eldest son—not known for his cooking skill—used it to impress his fiancée, now his wife. The technique works equally well with pork tenderloin, although we usually use a good dry white wine to deglaze the pan.

Protein per serving:
43 grams

Effective carb per serving:
5.9 grams

2 teaspoons coarse salt (plus a pinch, to taste)
2 teaspoons freshly ground black pepper (plus a pinch, to taste)
2 teaspoons garlic powder
1 tablespoon olive oil
1 pound beef tenderloin, trimmed
½ cup plus ¼ cup beef broth (divided for use)
1 sprig fresh rosemary
½ shallot
½ cup cabernet sauvignon
2 tablespoons unsalted butter

Preheat the oven to 500 degrees.

Combine the salt, pepper, and garlic powder in a ziplock bag.

Very lightly oil the tenderloin with olive oil.

Sprinkle the spice mixture liberally over all sides of the tenderloin and press it into the meat.

Heat 1 tablespoon of olive oil in a heavy ovenproof skillet or a roasting pan over medium-high heat.

Sear the tenderloin for a minute or so on all sides.

Add ¼ cup of the beef broth (to prevent smoking in the oven and to keep the meat moist) and the sprig of rosemary to the skillet.

Transfer the skillet to the oven and roast the tenderloin for 8 to 10 minutes.

Remove the skillet from the oven; transfer the tenderloin to a cutting board, cover with aluminum foil, and allow the meat to rest. You can prepare up to this point and hold the meat under the foil for at least 30 minutes.

MEDALLIONS
OF BEEF
TENDERLOIN
WITH CABERNET
REDUCTION
(continued)

Do not wash the skillet or discard the roasting juices and bits. With the skillet still hot, add the chopped shallot and cook for a minute or so. Add ½ cup of the beef broth to the skillet, scraping all the caramelized juices and bits with a spoon.

Add the cabernet sauvignon and bring to a boil to reduce the volume of the sauce by about half.

If you are delaying the final preparation, stop at this point, cover the skillet, and turn the heat off.

Just before serving, slice the tenderloin into ¾-inch to 1-inch medallions.

Return the skillet to medium-high heat, add the butter to the sauce, and allow it to melt. Taste and, if needed, adjust with a pinch of salt or pepper. Remove the rosemary sprig.

Return the medallions to the hot pan and gently warm them in the sauce for 30 seconds to 1 minute on each side for medium rare, or a bit longer until you reach the desired level of doneness.

Remove the medallions to a warmed platter or serving plate, pour the sauce over them, and serve.

Shepherd's Pie

SERVES 6

When our sons were home, we relied on one-dish meals like this one that we could assemble in advance, refrigerate, and heat quickly when we got home from work. This is perfect to feed hungry kids on a budget and will stretch easily if they surprise you with a friend or two for dinner.

Protein per serving:
27.2 grams

Effective carb per serving:
15.1 grams

3 tablespoons olive oil
1 medium onion, peeled and diced
2 cloves garlic, peeled and minced
½ red bell pepper, seeded and diced small
½ yellow bell pepper, seeded and diced small
1½ pounds ground sirloin (or very lean beef)
1 can (15 ounces) diced tomatoes
1 cup beef broth
1 tablespoon tomato paste
1 tablespoon ThickenThin not/Starch (see page 9) or
    2 teaspoons xanthan gum
1 cup white wine
½ teaspoon salt
½ teaspoon freshly ground black pepper
1 teaspoon chopped fresh tarragon or ½ teaspoon dried
½ cup frozen green peas
1 recipe prepared Creamed Fauxtatoes (page 150)
2 tablespoons grated Parmesan cheese

Heat the olive oil in a skillet over medium heat. Sauté the onion, garlic, and bell peppers until soft.

Add the ground meat and cook, stirring occasionally to brown evenly.

In a blender or a food processor, puree the canned tomatoes and set aside.

Meanwhile, in a small bowl, whisk together the broth, tomato paste, and ThickenThin.

Add the pureed tomatoes, broth mixture, wine, salt, pepper, and tarragon to the meat in the skillet and stir to combine thoroughly.

Stir in the peas and cook until the liquid in the pan reduces by at least half.

Transfer the meat mixture into a 2- or 2½-quart covered casserole dish and top with the Creamed Fauxtatoes. (If you wish to finish the casserole the next day, stop at this point and allow the casserole to cool sufficiently to refrigerate. Store, covered, overnight. Bring to room temperature before proceeding.)

Preheat the oven to 325 degrees.

Place the covered casserole into the oven and heat for about 25 minutes.

Remove the casserole from the oven and sprinkle on the Parmesan cheese. Place the dish, uncovered, under the broiler for a few minutes to brown the top. Serve immediately.

Luscious Lasagna

There seems to be nothing missing from this eminently satisfying lasagna except the extra carbs. You'll love it made the classic way with low-carb Impasta noodles, or try substituting leaves of steamed green cabbage or kale in place of noodles for a different taste. Although it looks like a complicated recipe with lots of ingredients, it's really very easy to do. Save time by making a double batch; it freezes well in individual portions and can be reheated in the microwave.

Protein per serving:
37 grams

Effective carb per serving:
8 grams

NOODLES
1 recipe Impasta dough (page 143)
1 tablespoon coarse salt

MEAT SAUCE
1 tablespoon extra-virgin olive oil
1 clove garlic, minced
½ onion, chopped
1 tablespoon minced fresh oregano
1 tablespoon minced fresh basil
1 bay leaf
¾ pound ground beef
½ pound Homemade Sage and Pepper Sausage (page 47) or commercial bulk sausage
2 tablespoons tomato paste
1 can crushed roasted tomatoes with juice

RICOTTA MIXTURE
2 cups ricotta (almost all of 1 large container)
2 tablespoons minced fresh flat-leaf parsley
1 tablespoon fresh minced oregano
½ teaspoon salt
½ teaspoon freshly ground black pepper
1 egg, beaten
¼ cup freshly grated Parmigiano Reggiano

ASSEMBLY

¼ cup prepared tomato sauce

½ pound mozzarella cheese, shredded (for layering)

¼ cup Parmigiano Reggiano (topping)

¼ cup shredded mozzarella (topping)

Prepare one recipe Impasta and roll into lasagna ribbons, using a pasta machine or rolling out by hand. Dry one half of the noodles for future use.

Make the meat sauce. Heat the olive oil in a large skillet over medium heat. Sauté the garlic, onion, and herbs for 4 to 5 minutes. Add the ground beef and sausage and cook another 15 minutes or until no pink remains in the meat. Spoon off the fat and add the tomato paste and crushed tomatoes, stirring to combine. Remove from the heat and set aside to cool.

Meanwhile, bring 2 quarts of water plus 1 tablespoon of coarse salt to a boil in a large covered pot.

In a bowl, make the ricotta mixture by combining the ricotta, parsley, oregano, salt, pepper, egg, and Parmesan cheese. Stir until thoroughly mixed. Set aside.

Drop the fresh lasagna noodles into the pot of boiling, salted water and cook 3 to 4 minutes until just tender. (Remember, they will cook again in the oven.)

TO ASSEMBLE

Preheat the oven to 350 degrees.

Ladle ½ of the meat sauce onto the bottom of a lightly oiled 9 × 13-inch baking dish or a small lasagna pan. Top with ½ of the ricotta mixture and ½ of the mozzarella reserved for layering.

Add a layer of cooked lasagna noodles, the remaining meat sauce, the remaining ricotta mixture, and the remaining layering mozzarella.

Top with the remaining lasagna noodles, the prepared tomato sauce, the grated Parmesan cheese, and the ¼ cup of shredded mozzarella.

Bake for about an hour.

Remove from the oven and let the lasagna rest for 20 to 30 minutes before cutting into six squares for serving.

Red Chile Rolled Enchiladas

SERVES 4

We've spent a lot of time in New Mexico, where, at restaurants, waiters will often pose the question: red, green, or Christmas? They're asking if you would like your dish topped with red chile, green chile, or both. We love our enchiladas with any of the above, although we're partial to the rich taste of beef, bison, or ostrich with red. If there's a chile wimp in the crowd, select a mild enchilada sauce and let the more adventurous shake as much hot chile sauce onto their serving as they can stand.

Protein per serving:
30.5 grams

Effective carb per serving:
7.9 grams

2 tablespoons olive oil
½ red onion, diced
1 clove garlic, minced
1 pound ground ostrich (or lean ground beef or bison, if you prefer)
1 tablespoon ground cumin
1 tablespoon ground chile powder
¼ teaspoon cayenne pepper (or to taste)
½ teaspoon salt
½ teaspoon freshly ground black pepper
8 small low-carb tortillas
1 can (about 15 ounces) commercial red chile enchilada sauce, mild or medium
1 package (about 1½ cups) shredded Mexican cheese (divided for use)

Preheat the oven to 375 degrees.

In a skillet, heat the olive oil over medium heat; sauté the onion and garlic until translucent but not brown.

Season the meat with the cumin, chili powder, cayenne, salt, and pepper, mixing thoroughly to distribute the spices evenly throughout.

Add the meat to the skillet, breaking it up to brown evenly.

Lightly oil a baking dish large enough to hold the 8 rolled enchiladas.

On a flat tortilla, place ⅛ of the seasoned cooked meat down the center; top with 1 tablespoon of the enchilada sauce and ⅛ cup of the shredded cheese. Roll up and place the tortilla, seam side down, in the baking dish. Repeat for the remaining 7 tortillas.

When all the enchiladas are placed in the baking dish, pour the remaining enchilada sauce over them and top with the remaining ½ cup of the shredded cheese.

You can cover and refrigerate the enchiladas at this point for baking within 24 hours; if you do, bring the dish to room temperature before baking.

Bake for 25 to 30 minutes until the cheese melts and the enchiladas are heated throughout.

VARIATION

Try the same recipe with ground chicken, pork, or turkey and green chile enchilada sauce.

Three-Alarm Chili

Big, beefy flavor and lots of heat is how we like our chili con carne, but if you don't like yours quite so spicy, simply dial down the heat. Feel free to start with just a dash of cayenne and adjust the seasonings to your liking. For the truly adventurous who like to break a sweat when they enjoy a bowl of chili, add an extra half teaspoon or more of cayenne and even throw a handful of chopped fresh or canned jalapeños on top.

Protein per serving:
39 grams

Effective carb per serving:
9.3 grams

2 pounds lean sirloin or bison steak

2 tablespoons olive oil

1 small yellow onion, peeled and diced

2 cloves garlic, peeled and minced

2 tablespoons chili powder

1 tablespoon ground cumin

½ teaspoon cayenne pepper (or to taste)

1 teaspoon salt

½ teaspoon freshly ground black pepper

1 cup sliced white button mushrooms, fresh or canned

1 can (4 ounces) diced green chili peppers

1 can (15 ounces) diced tomatoes

1 can (15 ounces) black soybeans, rinsed and drained

1 quart beef broth

1 cup dry red wine (optional)

4 tablespoons grated Mexican four-cheese blend

2 green onions, chopped

Place the meat into the freezer for 30 minutes to make it easier to cut into half-inch cubes.

In a large skillet or a soup pot, heat the olive oil over medium heat; add the onion and garlic and sauté until limp.

Add the meat, chili powder, cumin, cayenne, salt, and pepper and sauté until browned on all sides, about 4 to 5 minutes.

Add the mushrooms and sauté another few minutes until the mushrooms give up their juices.

Stir in the green chilies, tomatoes, and black soybeans.

Add the beef broth and wine, increase the heat to medium-high, and bring to a boil.

Reduce the heat and simmer, uncovered, for 45 minutes.

To serve, top each bowl with grated cheese, chopped fresh green onions, and for the adventurous, a tablespoon or two of sliced jalapeños.

White Chili

SERVES 6

While we've long been fans of the beefy red version, this southwestern take on the old classic draws its inspiration from the green chile stews of New Mexico, some of which are so hot you can't taste them. This one is milder, but feel free to ratchet up (or down) the heat to your liking with more (or less) cayenne. It's a great way to use up leftover pork roast, pork tenderloin, or even pork chops, but it's so delicious you might find yourself making extra servings of pork roast just to have the leftovers to use.

Protein per serving:
38 grams

Effective carb per serving:
12 grams

1 tablespoon olive oil
1 small yellow onion, peeled and diced
2 cloves garlic, peeled and minced
2 cans (15 ounces) yellow tomatoes
4 cups cooked and diced roast pork
1 teaspoon salt
1 teaspoon freshly ground black pepper
½ teaspoon cayenne pepper (or to taste)
2 tablespoons finely ground epazote (Mexican tea), if available*
2 teaspoons cumin
2 teaspoons fajita seasoning
2 cans (15 ounces) black soybeans, rinsed and drained
2 cans (4 ounces) green chili peppers, diced
1 quart chicken broth
2 green onions, chopped (for garnish)

*Epazote, also called Mexican tea, is a resinous herb that purportedly reduces the gas-forming nature of beans when cooked in recipes using them. It is usually available from retailers that carry a variety of Hispanic foods, spices, and herbs or through online spice sources. Its use is optional.

Heat the olive oil in a soup pot over medium heat. Sauté the onion and garlic until limp.

Meanwhile, puree the canned tomatoes in a blender or a food processor until nearly smooth and set aside.

To the soup pot, add the pork, salt, pepper, and spices, stirring to distribute the spices evenly, and continue to cook briefly.

Add the black soybeans, tomato puree, chilies, and chicken broth. Stir to combine. Bring to a boil, reduce the heat and simmer, uncovered, for 30 minutes to 1 hour to reduce the stock by about half and to thicken the chili. Stir occasionally to prevent sticking.

Serve with a garnish of chopped fresh green onions.

Spicy Southern Fried Chicken

SERVES 6

*Nothing calls up memories of a Southern childhood like a big plat-
ter of crispy fried chicken—the crunch of the crust, the juicy meat
beneath, the whole "finger-lickin' good" experience. Of course,
nobody could make it like Momma, but we think this lower-carb
version would make her proud.*

*Protein per
serving:*
61 grams
(Please note that
the gram counts
for this dish are an
average of ⅙ of a
chicken per per-
son; chickens,
however, don't
come equally
divided, but in
defined pieces, the
breasts larger and
the thighs smaller.)

*Effective carb
per serving:*
6.7 grams

LOW-CARB BREADING MIXTURE (MAKES 2 CUPS)
1 cup low-carb bread crumbs
1 cup almond flour
1 teaspoon salt
1 teaspoon freshly ground black pepper
1 teaspoon poultry seasoning
1 teaspoon paprika
¼ teaspoon cayenne pepper

CHICKEN PARTS
4 boneless chicken breast halves, with skin
4 chicken thighs, with skin
8 tablespoons coconut oil
4 eggs, beaten lightly

TO MAKE THE LOW-CARB BREADING MIXTURE

Place scraps or slices of stale, dry, low-carb white or wheat bread into
a blender. (If the bread is fresh, cut into cubes, place in a single layer
onto a baking sheet, and dry out in a 250-degree oven first.)

Pulse to pulverize the dry bread to medium-fine crumbs.

Thoroughly mix the bread crumbs with the almond flour, salt, pepper, poultry seasoning, paprika, and cayenne pepper.

TO BRINE THE CHICKEN

Although this step is optional, brining the chicken will make it moist
and flavorful. Wash the chicken pieces, place them into a bowl, sprinkle with Kosher salt, cover tightly, and refrigerate overnight. Before
cooking, rinse the chicken well and pat dry with paper towels.

Heat the oil in a heavy skillet over medium-low heat.

Put the low-carb breading mixture into a pie plate or a wide, shallow dish.

Put the beaten eggs into another pie plate or wide, shallow dish.

Dip the chicken first into the egg, then dredge in the crumbs to coat.

Working in batches if necessary to prevent overcrowding the pan, fry slowly, skin side down, until golden brown, 15 to 20 minutes.

Turn and cook on the other side, another 15 minutes or so, until a meat thermometer inserted into the thickest part of the meat registers an internal temperature of 165 degrees.

Remove the chicken from the pan and drain on a wire rack; alternatively, drain on a thick layer of paper towels, although this method will yield less crispy skin.

Barbecued Chicken Hot Wings

SERVES 8

Summer in the South means grilling outdoors—no added heat in the kitchen and no messy cleanup of pots and pans. Taught to us by an old Memphis barbecue aficionado, this recipe has been used by our family since our sons were kids. Tending the wings (always Mike's job) requires a good set of tongs, a good book to read, a tall gin and diet tonic or two, and patience, but the payoff is worth the effort. Make plenty; they'll go fast.

Protein per serving:
22.5 grams

Effective carb per serving:
0.2 gram

DIPPING SAUCE
1 cup water
½ cup olive oil
½ cup red wine vinegar
2 tablespoons chili powder
½ teaspoon cayenne pepper

WINGS
4 pounds chicken wings*
coarse salt and freshly ground black pepper to taste

TO MAKE THE SAUCE
Well in advance, mix all the ingredients together in a saucepan and bring to a boil.
   Continue to boil for 5 minutes.
   Remove from the heat and set aside.

TO GRILL THE WINGS
Bring a gas or a charcoal grill to medium-high heat.
   Meanwhile, cut the tips from the wings with a heavy knife or poultry shears.
   Rinse the wings and pat them dry with paper towels.
   Sprinkle the wings with salt and pepper.

*Allow about ½ pound of wings per person when adjusting the recipe. No need to make more sauce for even double this amount of wings.

Arrange the wings on the grate and cook them for 1 to 1½ hours, turning and rearranging them very frequently to keep them from burning, while allowing them to cook and slightly dry out. Don't stray far from the grill or the wings will burn.

When the wings look slightly dry, remove them from the grill with tongs and immediately dip them into the dipping sauce and place them onto a serving platter.

Serve immediately if possible. Although they will hold for up to 30 minutes tightly covered in foil in a warm oven, they'll lose some of their crispy texture.

Oven-Barbecued Hot Wings

SERVES 8

These oven-roasted hot wings retain all the taste of their flame-roasted-on-the-outdoor-grill cousins without the hassle of constant attention to prevent them from burning. They're super easy to make and weather independent. Now you can have a wingding in the dead of winter or on a rainy Saturday in spring.

Protein per serving:
22.5 grams

Effective carb per serving:
0.2 gram

DIPPING SAUCE
1 cup water
½ cup olive oil
½ cup red wine vinegar
2 tablespoons chili powder
½ teaspoon cayenne pepper

WINGS
4 pounds chicken wings*
coarse salt and freshly ground black pepper to taste

TO MAKE THE SAUCE

Well in advance, mix all the ingredients together in a saucepan and bring to a boil.

Continue to boil for 5 minutes.

Remove from the heat and set aside.

TO MAKE THE WINGS

Preheat the oven to 400 degrees.

Heat a grill pan over medium-high heat.

Meanwhile, cut the tips from the wings with a heavy knife or poultry shears.

Rinse the wings and pat them dry with paper towels.

Sprinkle the wings with salt and pepper.

Arrange the wings on the grill pan and cook them for about 5 minutes per side.

*Allow about ½ pound of wings per person when adjusting the recipe. No need to make more sauce for even double this amount of wings.

Remove the wings from the grill pan with tongs and arrange them on an oiled broiler pan.

Place the wings into the oven for 30 minutes.

Reduce the oven temperature to 350 degrees, flip all the wings over, and return them to the oven to cook for 30 minutes more.

Reduce the oven temperature to 200 degrees. Flip the wings again and cook them for another 30 to 45 minutes.

When ready to serve, remove the wings from the oven and immediately dip them into the dipping sauce and place them onto a serving platter.

Serve immediately if possible. Although they will hold for up to 30 minutes tightly covered in foil in a warm oven, they'll lose some of their crispy texture.

Green Chile Chicken Enchiladas

SERVES 8

In northern New Mexico, the traditional enchilada is made layered in a casserole, not rolled as is the custom in Mexico. We make this quick and easy recipe often for friends and family because everybody loves it and it's perfect for casual entertaining. All you need is a big salad and a pitcher of low-carb margaritas.

Protein per serving:
44 grams

Effective carb per serving:
9.3 grams

2 pounds boneless skinless chicken breast or chicken tenders
2 teaspoons coarse salt
2 teaspoons freshly ground black pepper
1 tablespoon ground cumin
½ to 1 teaspoon cayenne pepper
2 tablespoons olive oil
1 red onion, cut julienne-style
2 cloves garlic, minced
1 can (15 ounces) green chile enchilada sauce, medium heat
6 low-carb tortillas (small size)
1 package shredded Mexican cheese (organic if possible)

Cut the chicken into ½-inch cubes.
   Sprinkle it with salt, pepper, cumin, and cayenne.
   Heat the olive oil in a large skillet.
   Sauté the onion and garlic in the olive oil over medium-high heat until translucent.
   Add the chicken pieces and cook until opaque. Set aside.

ASSEMBLE THE LAYERED ENCHILADAS
Preheat the oven to 325 degrees.
   Coat the bottom of a 10- to 12-inch oblong baking dish or a small lasagna pan with ⅛ cup of green chile enchilada sauce.
   Cover the bottom of the pan with two tortillas, laid end to end.
   Build a layer using ½ of the chicken mixture, ⅓ of the cheese, and ⅓ of the remaining enchilada sauce.
   Add a second layer of two tortillas, laid end to end.
   Build the second layer using the remaining chicken and an additional ⅓ of the cheese and ⅓ of the enchilada sauce.

Cover with a last layer of two tortillas, laid end to end, and top with the remaining cheese and enchilada sauce.

Bake for 25 to 30 minutes until the cheese bubbles and melts.

Cool slightly before serving.

Chicken Potpie

SERVES 6

Kids and grown-ups alike will love the steaming comfort of this chicken potpie. It's filled with the traditional veggies, the creamy sauce, the chunks of chicken, and a crust that won't bust your carb budget. And what could be easier than a one-dish meal? It will keep, covered, in the refrigerator for a day or two and reheats nicely even in the microwave, making it a good grown-up lunch option, too.

Protein per serving:
22.5 grams

Effective carb per serving:
6 grams

1 recipe Tender Almond Pie and Tart Crust (page 207)
1 tablespoon olive oil
½ cup diced carrots
½ cup diced celery
¼ cup minced onion
½ teaspoon salt
½ teaspoon freshly ground black pepper
½ teaspoon poultry seasoning
2 cups chicken stock
1 tablespoon ThickenThin not/Starch (see page 9)
2 cups diced cooked chicken
½ cup frozen green peas
¼ cup heavy cream

Preheat the oven to 350 degrees.

Prepare the crust and roll it out large enough to completely cover the top of your baking dish.

Coat the bottom of a medium saucepan with the olive oil, place over medium heat, and add the carrots, celery, onion, salt, pepper, and poultry seasoning. Sauté until the onions are translucent and the vegetables have softened.

Pour in the chicken stock and bring to a boil.

Reduce the heat to low. Remove 2 tablespoons of the hot stock and add it to the ThickenThin, stirring to make a smooth mixture.

Add this mixture to the stock, whisking vigorously until the broth thickens.

Add the cooked chicken and frozen peas and continue to cook for about 5 more minutes on low heat. Stir in the cream and remove from the heat.

Pour the chicken mixture into a 2-quart baking dish or casserole and top with the piecrust, sealing it all the way around. Cut a steam vent or two in the center with a sharp knife.

Bake for 20 to 25 minutes until lightly browned.

Chicken Satay

SERVES 4

One or two of these skewers make a great appetizer; four or more can be a hearty, casual, Asian-inspired entrée. The number you can make depends only on the size of your grill or grill pan. If you're making large numbers for a party, be sure to hold them, tightly covered, in a warm oven (at least 160 degrees); serve them in a warming pan alongside a bowl of Thai Peanut Sauce.

Protein per serving:
44 grams

Effective carb per serving:
11 grams

1 pound boneless skinless chicken breast or tenders
2 recipes Thai Peanut Sauce, divided in half for use (page 176)

Brine the chicken breasts in a covered container in 1 quart of water plus ¼ cup of kosher salt for at least 2 hours in the refrigerator.

Soak 16 bamboo skewers (10 to 12 inches long) for 30 minutes.

Rinse the breasts and pat them dry with paper towels.

Pound the breasts flat until they're about ¼ inch thick.

Slice the meat on the diagonal into pieces about 1 inch wide.

Thread the pieces of chicken onto the skewers from side to side up the length of the slice to make a "wave" of chicken along the skewer.

Arrange the skewers in a baking dish and pour ½ (1 recipe) of the Thai Peanut Sauce over them, turning to coat all the sides in the sauce. Cover the skewers and refrigerate them for about 1 hour.

Grill the skewers over a medium-hot fire or on a grill pan over medium-high heat for 2 to 3 minutes per side. (Be sure to discard all the peanut sauce that remains in the dish once you have put the skewers on the grill; it has been in contact with the raw chicken and should not be eaten.)

Remove the skewers to a clean platter; pour the other half of the Thai Peanut Sauce into four small clean bowls for dipping.

Chicken Mushroom Packets

SERVES 4

Any recipe that's easy to make, can be assembled in advance, and demands minimal cleanup is a winner in our book. When our boys were still at home, we relied often on just such hobo supper meals. To save time, assemble the packets the night before, refrigerate them, and then pop them into the oven while you toss a salad and sauté some colorful veggies or make a batch of Creamed Fauxtatoes (page 150).

Protein per serving:
25 grams

Effective carb per serving:
1.3 grams

1 cup dried wild mushrooms, rehydrated, or 8 ounces canned sliced mushrooms
2 tablespoons olive oil (approximately)
1 teaspoon salt (divided in half for use)
1 teaspoon freshly ground black pepper (divided in half for use)
1 teaspoon rubbed sage (divided in half for use)
2 tablespoons unsalted butter, softened
1 tablespoon ThickenThin not/Starch (see page 9) or 2 teaspoons xanthan gum
½ cup heavy cream
4 thinly sliced boneless, skinless breast fillets*

Preheat the oven to 350 degrees.

If using dried mushrooms, rehydrate them in water for about 15 minutes until they plump.

Tear four 12-inch squares of aluminum foil and brush one side of them with a bit of olive oil.

In a small bowl, mix together the salt, pepper, and sage.

Rinse the fillets and pat them dry with paper towels. Then rub the fillets all over lightly with a little olive oil and sprinkle about half the salt, pepper, and sage mixture evenly on both sides. Place a fillet into the center of each piece of foil.

*Thinly sliced breast fillets are available at most markets. If you cannot find them, simply pound a boneless, skinless breast until it is about ¼ inch thick.

In a small bowl, cream together the butter, ThickenThin, and the remaining salt, pepper, and sage; then incorporate the cream to make a smooth, thick sauce.

Drain the mushrooms. If they are large, chop coarsely and fold them by hand into the cream mixture.

Divide this mushroom mixture evenly among the pieces of chicken.

Drizzle a bit more olive oil over each piece.

Make tight packets of each foil square by bringing the opposite corners to the center and crimping the foil at the four seams. (Refrigerate the meat if not cooking it right away. Bring it to room temperature before cooking.)

Place the packets onto a baking sheet and bake for about 30 minutes, until the chicken is fully cooked (to an internal temperature of 165 degrees.) Serve immediately.

Thai Red Chile Chicken

SERVES 4

Once, on a trip with a group of friends to the Florida coast, we happened upon a small roadside Thai restaurant and stopped in for a bite. The menu offered heat levels geared to the Tenderfoot, the Adventurous, or Native Thai. We chose mostly Adventurous selections but opted for one dish done Native Thai; it was honestly so hot you couldn't taste it. This dish is quite mild by comparison, but feel free to add more chile paste, a palmful of crushed red pepper, or a dash or five of Tabasco if you'd like to break a sweat.

Protein per serving:
48.8

Effective carb per serving:
4.7 grams
(Values are for the chicken dish only. Serving atop ½ cup of Spagaroni will add another 5.5 grams of carb per serving for a total of 10.3 grams.)

2 pounds boneless, skinless chicken breasts or tenders
½ teaspoon coarse salt
¼ teaspoon freshly ground black pepper
1 can (about 14 ounces) premium unsweetened coconut milk
2 tablespoons Thai roasted red chile paste
1 tablespoon Thai fish sauce
2 packets Splenda
½ cup frozen green peas
1 recipe Spagaroni (page 148)

Cut the chicken into bite-size chunks and season them lightly with salt and pepper.

Place the coconut milk into a large saucepan over medium heat; stir in the red chile paste and cook for about 5 minutes.

Add the fish sauce, Splenda, chicken pieces, and peas and cook for another minute or two.

Reduce the heat and simmer for another 10 minutes, stirring occasionally.

Serve atop a mound of Spagaroni in lieu of rice or pasta.

VARIATION

For Thai Red Chile Coconut Chicken Soup, cut the chicken smaller, add 2 cups of chicken stock when you add the fish sauce, omit the Spagaroni, and serve in bowls with a garnish of fresh cilantro.

Fish and Pepper Packets

SERVES 4

You'll love the island flavor of fish done this way. Even more, you'll love that it's easy to prepare and there's little to no cleanup. To serve this as a fun meal for kids or even guests, you can get a little artsy and tear the foil large enough to seal lengthwise and then form the ends of the packets to create the shape of a fish. To save time, prep the packets the night before, store them in the refrigerator, then bring them to room temperature and bake.

Protein per serving:
30 grams

Effective carb per serving:
4.4 grams

4 pieces (4 to 5 ounces each) of salmon, sea bass, or other firm-fleshed fish

1 to 2 tablespoons extra-virgin olive oil (approximately)

1 teaspoon salt (or to taste)

1 teaspoon freshly ground black pepper (or to taste)

½ teaspoon cumin

½ yellow bell pepper, seeded and coarsely diced

½ red bell pepper, seeded and coarsely diced

1 green poblano chili (or green bell pepper), seeded and sliced into 8 to 12 rings

2 medium zucchini, sliced lengthwise and diced

½ white onion, sliced

1 tablespoon minced fresh basil or 1 teaspoon dried

2 tablespoons minced fresh cilantro or 2 teaspoons dried

Preheat the oven to 425 degrees.

Rinse the fish and pat dry with paper towels. Remove the skin and any bones you can feel, running your hand along the length of each piece.

Tear four rectangles of aluminum foil large enough to make loose packets to hold the fish and peppers.

Lightly oil the central area of each of the pieces of foil.

Place a piece of fish into the center of each foil rectangle.

Sprinkle each piece of fish lightly with salt, pepper, and cumin.

Distribute ¼ of each type of pepper, zucchini, and onion evenly on each of the fish pieces.

Sprinkle the fish with the fresh or dried herbs.

Drizzle each serving with a little more olive oil.

Fold the foil ends together and crimp the middle and both ends to make a sealed packet.

Place all the packets onto a baking sheet and bake for 20 to 25 minutes.

Serve immediately.

Tilapia Soft Tacos

SERVES 4

Since they made their way from Baja up the coast of California, fish tacos have become a favorite healthy "fast food" in America. While we enjoy them most with our bare feet in the soft sand of a beach-side taqueria, they're delicious anytime, anywhere.

Protein per serving:
44 grams

Effective carb per serving:
9.2 grams

2 pounds tilapia filets
2 limes
¼ cup olive oil
2 cloves garlic, diced
2 tablespoons chopped fresh cilantro
1 teaspoon chile powder
1 teaspoon coarse salt
1 teaspoon freshly ground black pepper
¼ teaspoon cayenne pepper

SOFT TACOS
8 small low-carb tortillas, warmed
1 cup shredded iceberg lettuce
1 small tomato, seeded and diced
Mexican Cream (page 171), optional
Salsa Verde (page 64), optional

Cut the fish filets into chunks about 1 inch wide and 2 inches long.

Juice the 2 limes and put the juice, olive oil, garlic, cilantro, and all the spices into a large ziplock bag.

Put the fish chunks into the bag, seal tightly, turn over a few times to coat the fish, and marinate for at least 30 minutes in the refrigerator.

Allow the fish to come to room temperature before cooking.

Lightly oil a large skillet, a griddle, or a grill pan with coconut oil and melt over medium-high heat.

Cook the fish chunks about 3 minutes on each side, or until done (opaque but not dry).

Meanwhile, roll each tortilla in a sheet of paper towel and heat each one in the microwave for 20 seconds on high. Alternatively, warm the tortilla on the stove top burner briefly.

When the fish is cooked, divide it evenly among the warmed tortillas and top with the shredded lettuce, diced tomato, and a dollop of commercial or homemade Salsa Verde and Mexican Cream, if desired.

Seafood Casserole

SERVES 4

We love to entertain with this dish, since it can be prepared to a point, held in the refrigerator, and then reheated to bubbling while you and your guests enjoy drinks, nibbles, and conversation. The recipe easily multiplies for a bigger crowd and needs only a simple salad of interesting greens, warm loaves of Handmade Rye Bread (page 72), and a buttery Chardonnay, Sauvignon Blanc, or Pinot Blanc to make a truly memorable casual supper.

Protein per serving:
19.9 grams

Effective carb per serving:
9.9 grams

12 medium shrimp, shelled and deveined
12 sea scallops
6 tablespoons unsalted butter
3 cloves garlic, peeled and finely minced
2 cups sliced mushrooms
1 can diced tomatoes, drained
½ teaspoon coarse salt
½ teaspoon freshly ground black pepper
2 teaspoons paprika
1½ cups heavy cream
¼ cup low-carb bread crumbs*
¼ cup grated Parmigiano Reggiano

Preheat the oven to 325 degrees.

Wash the shrimp and scallops; trim off the tendon of the scallops, if necessary, and if they are very large, cut them into half or in thirds.

In a large skillet, melt the butter over medium heat. When it foams, add the garlic, mushrooms, and tomatoes and cook for a minute or two.

Season with the salt, pepper, and paprika. Stir to distribute the seasonings.

Add the cream, reduce the heat to medium-low, and cook until the cream thickens, about 3 minutes.

*Save the heels and any trimmings from commercial low-carb bread or use new slices lightly toasted or left out for a day. Process by pulsing in a food processor to make low-carb bread crumbs.

Add the shrimp and scallops and continue to cook for another minute.

Transfer the seafood mixture into a lightly buttered 1-quart casserole or 4 individual ramekins. You may hold the cooled casserole, covered, for up to 24 hours in the refrigerator at this point. Bring the casserole to room temperature before resuming.

Sprinkle the bread crumbs and Parmesan cheese evenly over the casserole(s) and bake until bubbly and golden, about 20 minutes for the ramekins and about 30 minutes for a single, larger casserole.

Crab Cakes

SERVES 4

From our time spent living or working on the coasts of both New England and California, we've come to really love good crab cakes. We eat small ones as appetizers and larger ones for lunch or dinner entrées, and we even use them in place of English muffins as a platform for the eggs in a seafood variation of eggs Benedict as they do at one of our favorite hangouts at the Santa Barbara harbor.

Protein per serving:
29.6 grams

Effective carb per serving:
4.4 grams

1 pound fresh lump crabmeat
1 egg
¼ cup minced red or yellow bell pepper
2 green onions, minced
¼ cup Basic Blender Mayonnaise (page 169)
1 tablespoon Dijon mustard
¼ teaspoon salt (or to taste)
¼ teaspoon freshly ground black pepper (or to taste)
½ cup plus 2 tablespoons low-carb bread crumbs* (divided for use)
2 tablespoons unsalted butter
2 tablespoons olive or coconut oil
½ cup almond meal
1 teaspoon curry powder
1 lemon, cut in wedges (for garnish)

Pick over the crabmeat to remove any cartilage.

In a bowl, combine the crabmeat, egg, bell pepper, green onions, mayonnaise, mustard, salt, pepper, and about 2 tablespoons of the bread crumbs; use another tablespoon or two if needed to bind the mixture. Refrigerate the crab mixture for about 30 minutes if possible.

When ready to cook the cakes, heat the butter and olive oil in a large skillet over medium-high heat.

*Save the heels and any trimmings from commercial low-carb bread or use new slices lightly toasted or left out for a day. Process by pulsing in a food processor to make low-carb bread crumbs.

Make a dredging mixture of the remaining ½ cup of bread crumbs, the almond meal, and the curry powder.

Form the crab mixture into 4 large or 8 small cakes, and when the butter foams, dredge each cake in the bread-crumb mixture and cook until golden brown, 4 to 5 minutes per side. Turn very gently to avoid breaking the cake.

Garnish the cakes with the lemon wedges and serve immediately.

A-Lot-Like-Lacquered Salmon

SERVES 4

At Trios, a favorite restaurant in Little Rock, Arkansas, where we lived and worked for many years, a signature entrée is the original sweet and peppery version of this dish. When we're in town, we never fail to visit our good friends at Trios, and if we feel like a bit of a carb splurge, we order the salmon prepared this way. We don't get back there as much as we'd like, so we developed a lower-carb impression of their delectable dish.

Protein per serving:
34.9 grams

Effective carb per serving:
7 grams

SALSA GARNISH

4 green onions, chopped
2 tablespoons freshly grated gingerroot
¼ teaspoon garlic powder
½ teaspoon cumin
½ teaspoon coarse salt
1 lime, juice and zest
1 cup dry white wine
2 tablespoons chopped fresh cilantro
1 teaspoon aged balsamic vinegar
¼ cup olive oil

SALMON

2 tablespoons peanut or coconut oil
4 tablespoons granular Splenda
4 tablespoons finely ground black pepper
4 salmon fillets (about 6 ounces each), rinsed and patted dry

TO MAKE THE SALSA

In a small saucepan over medium-high heat, combine all the ingredients except the cilantro, balsamic vinegar, and olive oil and bring the mixture to a boil; reduce the heat to medium and cook, uncovered, to reduce the volume of the liquid by about half.

Remove the salsa from the heat, stir in the cilantro and balsamic vinegar, and set aside until serving time. Just before serving, whisk in the olive oil.

TO PREPARE THE SALMON

Put the peanut oil into a large, heavy skillet over high heat and tip in all directions to evenly coat the bottom.

In a shallow bowl, thoroughly mix the Splenda and black pepper.

Lightly brush both sides of each salmon fillet with olive oil and dredge in the Splenda-pepper mixture to evenly coat.

Carefully place the fillets into the hot oiled skillet and let them cook, undisturbed, for 4 minutes. Be aware that you may create some smoke here. Flip the fish and cook the remaining side for 3 to 5 minutes to your desired level of doneness.

Remove the fillets onto a serving plate, drizzle some of the salsa over them, and pass the remaining salsa around the table.

Shrimp Quesadilla

SERVES 1

The advent of good-tasting low-carb tortillas made such dishes an easy proposition for the low-carb dieter. This island twist on the old standard cheese quesadilla is our daughter-in-law's favorite. The recipe is for one, but it easily multiplies for an impromptu lunch or supper. Delicious served with a side of Mango Salsa (page 173) or Salsa Verde (page 64) and a dab of Mexican Cream (page 171) or sour cream.

Protein per serving:
59 grams
(This is a hearty portion of protein, contributed mainly by the cheese. Smaller appetites may wish to reduce the cheese to ¼ cup, which will reduce the protein grams to 41, or simply eat half a quesadilla.)

Effective carb per serving:
11.4 grams

1 large (burrito size) low-carb flour tortilla
½ cup grated Mexican four-cheese blend
20 cooked rock shrimp, rinsed
1 tablespoon canned diced green chili peppers

Heat a griddle or a large skillet and warm the tortilla briefly on one side.

Flip it over and scatter the cheese over half of the circle. Top the cheese with a scattering of shrimp and diced chilies.

When the cheese has melted, fold the empty half of the tortilla over the filling and press slightly to seal it closed.

Transfer the tortilla onto a cutting board and slice the half-moon into wedges for serving.

CHAPTER 6

◇ ◇ ◇

Accompaniments: Veggies and Side Dishes

Sautéed Broccoli with Sesame Fire Butter

Sautéed Cauliflower with Garlic Herb Butter

Onions au Gratin

◇   ◇   ◇

◇　◇　◇

The cliché criticism of carb-controlled diets involves a perceived dearth of fruits and vegetables. While that sentiment makes for a snappy sound bite on talk shows, nothing could be further from the truth. Properly followed, a low-carb diet contains a wealth of colorful fruits and vegetables, dark-green leafies, tender shoots, and savory roots. In fact, as we've always prescribed in our low-carb recommendations, it is in the produce section where people should spend the bulk of their carbohydrate bucks; that's true both in the earliest stages of corrective dieting and later on in maintenance, when the restrictions on carb intake liberalize, allowing for an even larger and more varied selection.

Most of the colorful members of the veggie tribe are naturally low in carbohydrate, rich in fiber, and filled with health-promoting antioxidants, vitamins, and minerals. In this category we include artichokes, asparagus, broccoli, cauliflower, celery, cucumbers, eggplant, flageolets (green kidney beans), garlic, green beans, greens, herbs, jicama, mushrooms, okra, peppers, pumpkin, radishes, rhubarb, soybeans, sprouts, squashes of all types, tomatoes, and turnips. All of these foods work just fine in reasonable portions, without any change in their common preparation methods. One obvious exception would be not to deep-fry them in a flour, cornmeal, or traditional batter crust. Even beets, carrots, parsnips, and onions, while they do contain a bit more sweetness, fit in nicely with a low-carb eating plan. You'll see we haven't included dozens of recipes detailing their use, because there are already plenty of cookbooks that contain those recipes. (One of our favorites is Deborah Madison's *Vegetarian Cooking for Everyone*, which, while not geared to carb grams, gives some of the most delicious recipes for vegetable side dishes known to us. When a vegetable gets into Deborah's hands, it just knows what to do.) You'll find a few standard veggie recipes here—notably Sautéed Broccoli with Sesame Fire Butter and Sautéed Cauliflower with Garlic Herb Butter and Roasted Baby Vegetables. These general techniques can be applied to almost any fresh colorful vegetable, and we encourage you to enjoy a wide and interesting variety of them—sautéed, steamed, grilled, roasted, or raw.

What we've mainly tried to include here are some methods for replacing the familiar look of the plate. Therein lies the main problem that we who choose to control our carb intake face in selecting side dishes to accompany the protein on our plates. The difficulty arises not from the vegetable world but from the false vegetables (really starches) and the grains. As a society, we've become conditioned to expect a big mound of potatoes, rice, pasta, or beans on every dinner plate, and breaking that habit may take a little effort. To ease that struggle, you'll find some delicious vegetable impostors here. Take the Creamed Fauxtatoes or Fauxtatoes au Gratin, for instance; at our house, we've come to prefer these recipes prepared with celery root, to the potatoes we enjoyed years ago. With a third of the carb grams and half of the calories of potatoes, celery root really does give you all the pleasure and none of the guilt. You'll find more information about celery root in the introduction to chapter 4.

By enjoying a cornucopia of fresh and colorful veggies, you will help us prove that a healthy low-carb diet is a lot more than just meat, bacon, cheese, and butter. The fact that you'll also be doing something really good for your health is a happy bonus.

Impasta (Almond Flour Pasta Dough)

SERVES 6 TO 12*

This pasta, unlike its fully wheat-based kin, is very hearty and filling thanks to its high protein content. All by itself, it provides enough protein for a meal even without a meat or cheese sauce. That makes it a great choice, dressed simply with a tomato sauce, for those finicky young eaters in the family. Great tossed just with butter, herbs, and Parmigiano Reggiano or dressed with your favorite sauce from marinara to alfredo; don't forget to count any extra carbs the sauce will contribute.

Protein per serving (for 6):
33.9 grams

Effective carb per serving (for 6):
6.7 grams

1 cup almond flour
½ cup whey protein powder
⅓ cup vital wheat gluten
½ cup whole-wheat flour
1 teaspoon fine salt
3 eggs

IMPOSTOR FLOUR
2 tablespoons whey protein powder
2 tablespoons almond flour
1 tablespoon xanthan gum

Combine the dry ingredients in a mixing bowl.

In a separate small container, lightly beat the eggs.

Make a well in the center of the flour mixture, pour in the beaten egg, and with a fork begin to stir from the center, bringing the dry ingredients into the wet ingredients until you have completely incorporated the flours.

Turn the ball of dough onto a surface lightly dusted with the impostor flour. Take over by hand and knead the pasta dough for 2 to 3 minutes, incorporating about 2 tablespoons of the impostor flour as needed to achieve a smooth, elastic, but not sticky, dough.

Wrap the dough in plastic wrap and allow it to rest for 20 minutes before processing further into the desired shape with a pasta machine or rolling out by hand and cutting into fettuccine or lasagna noodles or sheets for making ravioli.

*This recipe will make enough fettuccine or spaghetti for about 6 hearty servings or 8 side dish servings, or lasagna noodles sufficient for 12 servings.

BBQ Baked Black Soybeans

SERVES 6

Good Southern barbecue just isn't the same without a heap of tangy, sweet baked beans on the side, but their high-carb cost precludes having them . . . or at least having a decent-size portion of them very often. The black soybean, higher in protein and fiber and lower in starch, makes it possible to enjoy baked beans once again. We think these have just the right balance of sweetness, tang, and spice, but feel free to experiment with the amounts of Splenda, vinegar, mustard, and spice to re-create the taste you love.

Protein per serving:
11.6 grams

Effective carb per serving:
8 grams

1 small onion
1 clove garlic
4 slices bacon
½ cup low-carb tomato catsup
1 tablespoon ThickenThin not/Starch (see page 9)
1 tablespoon tomato paste
1 tablespoon red wine vinegar
6 packets Splenda
1 tablespoon Dijon mustard
½ teaspoon coarse salt
½ teaspoon freshly ground black pepper
¼ teaspoon cayenne pepper
2 cans (approximately 15 ounces each) black soybeans, rinsed and drained

Preheat the oven to 325 degrees.

Peel and slice the onion; peel and mince the garlic.

Dice 2 of the bacon slices.

In a small bowl, whisk together the catsup, ThickenThin, tomato paste, vinegar, Splenda, mustard, salt, pepper, and cayenne pepper.

Place the beans into an ovenproof casserole; pour the catsup mixture over the black soybeans; add the garlic, onion, and diced bacon and stir to combine the ingredients thoroughly.

Lay the remaining bacon slices across the top of the beans and bake for at least 30 minutes. Finish under the broiler for 2 to 3 minutes to crisp the top slices of bacon, if desired.

Serve warm; the beans will keep for up to 30 minutes, covered, in a warm oven or over a pot of simmering water.

Festive Frijoles

SERVES 4

A riot of colors and textures make these beans visually appealing, but they're delicious, too. The flavors pair well with Mexican and Southwestern entrées as well as Caribbean food. Easy to make and packed with protein and antioxidants, they're sure to please both the discriminating palate and the health-conscious mind.

Protein per serving:
8.7 grams

Effective carb per serving:
6.8 grams

1 tablespoon coconut oil
1 small red onion, diced
2 cans black soybeans, rinsed and drained
1 can (about 15 ounces) diced tomatoes
1 small can (4 ounces) diced roasted green chili peppers
¼ teaspoon cumin
¼ teaspoon roasted garlic powder
¼ teaspoon freshly ground black pepper
¼ teaspoon salt
¼ teaspoon cayenne pepper (optional)

Melt the coconut oil in a medium to large saucepan over medium heat.

Sauté the onion until translucent.

Add all the remaining ingredients and stir to combine.

Bring briefly to a boil, reduce the heat to low, and cook, stirring occasionally, for about 20 minutes until heated through and thickened.

If necessary, mash a few of the beans with a potato masher or a fork to thicken the juices. Serve hot.

Refried Black Soybeans

SERVES 4

These tasty and smooth beans make a delicious side dish to accompany any Mexican or Southwestern entrée without the heavy carb load of the original pinto bean version. They're delicious, too, as a bean burrito filling or wrapped in a low-carb tortilla with some cheese, and they even make a great bean dip.

Protein per serving:
8.6 grams

Effective carb per serving:
3.8 grams

1 can (15 ounces) black soybeans
½ teaspoon salt
½ teaspoon freshly ground black pepper
½ teaspoon cumin
cayenne pepper to taste
1 teaspoon epazote (Mexican tea), if available*
1 tablespoon coconut oil or lard
1 clove garlic, minced
¼ red onion, finely diced

GARNISH
1 tablespoon freshly grated asiago cheese
1 tablespoon Mexican Cream (page 171)
8 to 12 fresh cilantro leaves

Drain the black soybeans and mash with a fork to make a thick paste.
Add the salt, pepper, and spices and combine.
In a skillet, melt the coconut oil over medium-high heat.
Sauté the garlic and onion until translucent.
Add the mashed bean-and-spice mixture to the skillet.
Heat the mixture through.
Top each serving with a flourish of Mexican Cream, a sprinkle of grated cheese, and a bit of fresh cilantro.

*Epazote, also called Mexican tea, is a resinous herb that purportedly reduces the gas-forming nature of beans when cooked in recipes using them. It is usually available from retailers that carry a variety of Hispanic foods, spices, and herbs or through online spice sources. Its use is optional.

Butternut Squash Casserole

This recipe is an adaptation of the delicious candied sweet potato casserole that Aunt Nell always brought to family gatherings at Thanksgiving or Christmas. The taste and texture are just the same, but using butternut squash instead of candied yams makes the carb count far lower. Aunt Nell topped her casserole with real toasted marshmallows, and the advent of low-carb marshmallows makes that treat possible but optional. To our mind it's just as good without them.

Protein per serving:
1 gram

Effective carb per serving:
8 grams

2 medium butternut squash
2 tablespoons unsalted butter
2 teaspoons cinnamon
1 packet Splenda
1 teaspoon coarse salt
½ teaspoon freshly ground black pepper
10 to 15 Handmade Marshmallows (page 225), optional*

Preheat the oven to 400 degrees.

Cut the stem end from each squash, halve it lengthwise, remove the seeds, and place the cleaned squash halves into a roasting pan.

Place the butter, cinnamon, Splenda, and spices into the cavities, dividing the ingredients equally among the four squash halves.

Roast the squash for about an hour until very soft.

Allow the squash to cool slightly and scrape the cooked pulp into a blender or a food processor.

Pulse until smooth.

Taste for seasoning and adjust to your liking.

Turn the mixture into an ovenproof baking dish.

Return to the oven at 325 degrees for 15 to 20 minutes to warm through.

Serve immediately or hold, covered, in a warm oven or over a pan of simmering water for up to 30 minutes

Top with low-carb marshmallows, if desired, and place under the broiler for 2 to 3 minutes to brown the marshmallows.

*Low-carb marshmallows are available at many low-carb specialty stores and online if you don't want to make your own. Be aware that carb counts and ingredients vary, so read the label carefully.

Spagaroni

SERVES 4

Depending on how finely you chop, this recipe is a little bit like spaghetti, a little bit like Rice-A-Roni, or a little bit like soba noodles—and a lot low carb. Serve it as a side dish or as a rice or noodle substitute for Asian-inspired dishes. Spice it up with a little oregano or basil and it becomes a spaghetti-like base for your favorite pasta sauce.

Protein per serving:
0.8 gram

Effective carb per serving:
5.5 grams

1 spaghetti squash (about 3 pounds)
1 tablespoon olive oil
¼ red onion, peeled and diced
1 clove garlic, peeled and minced
½ green bell pepper, seeded and diced
½ red bell pepper, seeded and diced
¼ teaspoon salt
¼ teaspoon freshly ground black pepper

With a sharp knife and great care, remove the stem end from the spaghetti squash as close to the stem as possible.

Split the squash lengthwise and remove the seeds and stringy pith with a spoon.

Place the squash halves cut side down into a microwave-safe baking dish, add 1 tablespoon of water, cover tightly with a lid or plastic wrap, and microwave on high until tender, about 8 minutes.

Meanwhile, heat the olive oil in a skillet over medium heat. Add the onion and garlic and sauté until translucent. Add the peppers, season with salt and pepper, and sauté until crisp-tender. Remove the skillet from the heat, leaving the contents undisturbed.

When the squash is cool enough to handle, use a fork to scrape the "spaghetti" strands from the shell and onto a cutting board.

Coarsely chop the strands to make ½-inch pieces. (Leave the strands uncut if you seek a more noodlelike presentation.)

Place the skillet with the onions and peppers back over medium heat, add the chopped squash to the skillet, and stir to combine. Heat through.

Green Pea and Asparagus Casserole

SERVES 6

This low-carb take on an old family recipe always finds its way to our table at Thanksgiving and Christmas. Its silky and flavorful sauce can turn even the most vegetable averse into a green pea lover. Doubly delicious made with cooked fresh peas and asparagus, but the canned ones, as specified here, will do fine.

Protein per serving:
6.3 grams

Effective carb per serving:
6.3 grams

1 can (14 ounces) small green peas
1 can (about 14 ounces) green asparagus spears
2 tablespoons unsalted butter
2 tablespoons ThickenThin not/Starch (see page 9) or
    1 teaspoon xanthan gum
½ cup heavy cream
½ cup shredded cheddar cheese
½ teaspoon coarse salt
½ teaspoon freshly ground black pepper

Preheat the oven to 325 degrees.

Drain the peas and asparagus and reserve 1 cup of their liquid.

Put the butter into a 1-quart saucepan over medium heat.

Sprinkle the ThickenThin over the butter and mash with the tines of a fork to combine.

Add 2 to 3 tablespoons of the reserved pea and asparagus juices and whisk with the butter to make a smooth paste.

Add the remaining pea and asparagus juices and whisk until smooth.

Add the heavy cream, cheese, salt, and pepper. Continue to heat and allow the sauce to thicken slightly. If the sauce remains too thin, you may sprinkle on and whisk in another teaspoon or two of the ThickenThin.

Place a thin coating of the cheese sauce onto the bottom of a 2-quart casserole or a loaf pan, top with half the peas, half the asparagus spears, and half the remaining cheese sauce. Repeat the layers with the other half of the peas, asparagus, and sauce.

Bake for about 30 minutes until heated through.

Creamed Fauxtatoes (Celery Root Puree)

SERVES 6

As creamy and comforting as the potato version with far fewer carbs per serving, these delicious veggies are preferable to potatoes, we think, in both texture and flavor. At our house, they've earned the place of honor once held by mashed potatoes, rice, and polenta.

Protein per serving:
1.9 grams

Effective carb per serving:
8 grams

2 medium celery roots
1 teaspoon coarse salt
2 tablespoons unsalted butter, melted
2 to 3 tablespoons half-and-half
freshly ground black pepper (to taste)
salt to taste (optional)

TO PREPARE THE CELERY ROOT

Trim the top and base of the celery root with a knife. Remove the peel with a sturdy vegetable peeler. Rinse the peeled celery root. Dice the root into ½ to 1-inch pieces.

Put the prepared root into a medium saucepan, covered with water.

Add the salt to the water, cover, and bring to a boil.

Cook over medium-high heat for 12 to 15 minutes until fork tender, then drain.

Place the cooked celery root into a blender or a food processor.

Add the melted butter and a couple of tablespoons of half-and-half.

Blend or process until smooth. Pulse or blend on low for short intervals, turn the machine off, remove the lid, and use a spatula to scrape down the sides and push any unblended pieces to the bottom. Replace the lid and blend again. Repeat until the puree is smooth and creamy. Add more half-and-half by the tablespoon, only if necessary to thin the puree to the desired consistency.

Grind in fresh pepper to taste; add salt to taste, if desired.

Serve immediately or put in an ovenproof dish, cover, and hold on warm (180 degrees) for up to 1 hour in the oven or over a pan of simmering water.

Fauxtatoes au Gratin

SERVES 6

"Comfort in a casserole" best describes this dish. If you're a fan of the original potato-based number, you're going to love this creamy, cheesy version. Celery root, with about a third the usable carbs and half the calories of potatoes, works perfectly as a substitute. We love it with blue cheese, as specified here, but it would work just as well with grated Parmesan, Gruyère, cheddar, fontina, or any other cheese that melts smoothly.

Protein per serving:
7.2 grams

Effective carb per serving:
10 grams
(The carb value for this healthy portion is perfect for transition and maintenance carb levels. At the beginning stages of a low-carb diet, simply eat half a portion, which will still be a filling amount.)

2 large celery roots, peeled and sliced (⅛ inch thick)
¼ teaspoon salt
¼ teaspoon freshly ground black pepper
1 cup crumbled blue cheese (Gorgonzola, Stilton, Danish, or Roquefort)
1 cup heavy cream

Preheat the oven to 350 degrees.

Lightly oil a 1-quart casserole (a 9 × 6-inch loaf pan works well).

Place about half of the celery root slices into the dish, completely covering the bottom; season them with some of the salt and pepper.

Top this layer with about half of the cheese and drizzle half of the cream evenly over the layer.

Repeat with a second layer of celery root, salt and pepper, cheese, and cream and cover tightly with aluminum foil.

Bake for 35 to 40 minutes or until a knife slides easily through all the layers.

Remove the foil and bake for another 10 to 15 minutes to brown the top. Serve immediately.

Oven-Roasted Celery Root with Rosemary and Garlic

SERVES 6

This recipe is an adaptation of one of our favorite potato dishes. It's got all the taste of the original with a fraction of the carb load that prevented our having the potato version very often. The celery root comes out of the roasting oven crispy and brown but soft in the center, just the way potatoes did, and it fills the kitchen with the pungent aroma of rosemary and garlic.

Protein per serving:
1.7 grams

Effective carb per serving:
8 grams

2 medium celery roots
2 tablespoons olive oil
2 cloves garlic, minced
3 to 4 sprigs fresh rosemary, finely minced, or 2 teaspoons dried
½ teaspoon salt
½ teaspoon freshly ground black pepper

Preheat the oven to 350 degrees.

Peel the celery roots and cut them into 1-inch cubes.

Place them in a single layer into a shallow baking pan and drizzle the olive oil over them.

Sprinkle the garlic, rosemary, salt, and pepper and toss with your fingers to distribute the seasonings evenly.

Roast for about 30 minutes. Shake the pan or stir with a spoon to redistribute the pieces and return to the oven to roast for another 30 minutes until the celery roots are soft and begin to brown slightly.

Smashed Just Like Potatoes

SERVES 4

So creamy and buttery, with bits of red potato skin running all through, these impostors are hard to tell from the real McCoy. We not only love them for their yummy taste, but since cauliflower is filled with sulforaphane (a cancer-fighting phytochemical), we revel in their bigger nutritional bang for the carb buck. At our house, we've come to prefer them to potatoes.

Protein per serving:
3.6 grams

Effective carb per serving:
5.4 grams

1 large head cauliflower
3 to 4 small red potatoes (peel only)
1 slice bacon, finely diced
1 tablespoon olive oil
½ teaspoon salt
½ teaspoon freshly ground black pepper
2 tablespoons unsalted butter, melted
2 tablespoons heavy cream

Wash and trim the outer leaves from the cauliflower.

Slice the head in half and then slice the halves into ½-inch slices.

Break the slices up, place them into a microwave-safe bowl, add about ⅛ cup of water, cover tightly, and microwave on high for 6 minutes.

Remove the dish, carefully open the cover to let the steam escape, and stir. Replace the cover and continue to microwave on high for another 2 to 3 minutes until the cauliflower pieces are very soft.

Meanwhile, wash and peel the red potatoes, removing as little flesh as possible. Save the peelings and discard the flesh of the potatoes or save them for a different use. Coarsely chop the peels.

Fry the diced bacon in a small skillet to render the grease. Add the olive oil. Over medium to medium-high heat, sauté the potato peels until soft. Season to taste with salt and pepper.

Drain the cooked cauliflower as thoroughly as possible and transfer to a blender or a food processor.

Add the melted butter and heavy cream.

Puree in pulses or on a low setting in short bursts. After each short burst, stop the machine, and with the motor off, use a spatula to scrape down the sides, pushing the chunks toward the bottom.

Resume processing in pulses or bursts, repeating as many times as necessary to obtain a smooth puree. Add a bit more cream if needed to achieve the desired consistency.

Spoon the puree into a heatproof serving bowl. Add the fried potato skins to the puree and stir to combine.

Serve immediately or hold in the heatproof bowl, covered, in a warm oven or over a pan of simmering water for up to 30 minutes.

Old-Time Southern Collards

SERVES 4

In the South, boiled or sautéed greens of all types accompany many meals. Each variety has its own distinctive taste; collards have an earthy, rich flavor. This cooking method will work best for any of the tougher large greens, such as collards, turnip greens, mustard greens, and kale. Simple sautéing works better for tender greens such as spinach. To brighten the flavor, be sure to sprinkle on the pickled pepper juice—what at our house was called "pepper sauce"—or a little vinegar before serving.

Protein per serving:
5 grams

Effective carb per serving:
3.4 grams

6 slices bacon
2 large bunches fresh collard greens
2 teaspoons coarse salt
1 teaspoon freshly ground black pepper
1 small jar medium or hot pickled peppers and their juice

In a large stockpot, bring about 4 quarts of water to a boil.

Meanwhile, in a skillet, cook the bacon until crisp and remove it to paper towels to drain. Add the hot bacon grease from the skillet to the stockpot water.

Thoroughly wash the greens, rinse, drain, and repeat twice to remove all sand and grit.

Remove all stems and cut out all large tough stem veins from the leaves with a sharp knife.

Roughly chop the leaves into 4 to 6 pieces each and add to the boiling water.

Add the salt and pepper.

Return the greens to a boil, cook for about 10 minutes, then reduce the heat to a simmer. Cover and slowly cook the greens for about 45 more minutes until quite tender.

When the bacon is cool, crumble and reserve it.

Chop 3 or 4 pickled peppers and reserve.

Drain the greens.

Place the cooked greens into a large serving bowl, top with the crumbled bacon and chopped peppers, sprinkle on a tablespoon or two of the pickled pepper juice, and toss to combine. Serve immediately.

Roasted Baby Vegetables

SERVES 6

One of the least fussy ways to get a beautiful and colorful pile of vegetables on your plate is to use baby vegetables, which don't even require being cut up. We love to roast them in a big batch in the oven, so that we'll have some for a second night or to use in making an extra-quick pot of soup. If you can't find baby vegetables, use the grown-up ones and simply chunk them into similar-size pieces. *

Protein per serving:
5.2 grams

Effective carb per serving:
11.1 grams

12 baby zucchini
12 baby pattypan (scallop) squash
12 baby eggplants
2 pints cherry tomatoes
24 large stalks asparagus
6 cloves garlic, peeled, whole
3 tablespoons olive oil
1 teaspoon salt
1 teaspoon freshly ground black pepper
1 tablespoon finely chopped fresh flat-leaf parsley
3 green onions, chopped

Preheat the oven to 350 degrees.

Wash and dry the vegetables and put them into a roasting pan sufficiently large to hold them all in a roughly single layer.

Sprinkle them with the olive oil, salt, pepper, and parsley and toss to coat evenly.

Roast the vegetables for about 30 minutes, stirring occasionally to produce more even cooking. Test for tenderness and cook a bit longer if not quite tender.

Top with a sprinkling of fresh green onions and serve.

*Estimate that you will need 1 mature vegetable for every 4 baby vegetables specified. In the case of eggplant, substitute 1 large globe eggplant or 3 slender Japanese eggplants for 4 baby eggplants.

Sautéed Broccoli with Sesame Fire Butter

SERVES 6

Broccoli is a carb bargain and a real nutritional powerhouse, filled with vitamins, minerals, and sulforaphane. While many people share the elder president Bush's dislike for broccoli, this recipe is a preparation that's sure to win converts.

Protein per serving:
2.5 grams

Effective carb per serving:
1.9 grams

1 medium head broccoli (about 6 cups florets)
1 teaspoon olive oil
¼ cup water
2 tablespoons Sesame Fire Butter (page 174)

Rinse the broccoli well. Trim away the thick stem of the broccoli where it meets the thinner stalks and separate the florets, leaving a stem about 1½ inches long. Peel the thick stem and dice it. Set aside. Cut the florets in half lengthwise and then split lengthwise again (and again for large florets) to make ½-inch-thick pieces containing both florets and stems. This method will yield bite-size pieces that cook quickly and evenly—no mushy tops and undercooked stems.

Lightly oil a skillet with the olive oil and warm it on medium-high heat for about a minute. Remove from the heat, add the broccoli and the water, cover tightly, and return to high heat. Cook, shaking the skillet now and again, for about 4 minutes until the broccoli is tender and the water is gone.

Uncover the skillet, turn off the heat, add the Sesame Fire Butter, and allow it to melt. Toss the broccoli to coat evenly and serve.

Sautéed Cauliflower with Garlic Herb Butter

SERVES 6

Filled with vitamins, minerals, and cancer-fighting antioxidants but really low in useable carb, cauliflower is a low-carb dieter's friend. Although it makes a great substitute for potatoes in many dishes, it's delicious in its own right. Whether you're a fan or a skeptic, this tasty preparation is sure to please.

Protein per serving:
2.1 grams

Effective carb per serving:
2.9 grams

1 medium head cauliflower (about 6 cups florets)
1 teaspoon olive oil
½ teaspoon salt
¼ cup water
2 tablespoons Garlic Herb Butter (page 175)

Rinse the cauliflower well. Trim away the thick stem and leaves of the cauliflower where it meets the thinner stalks and separate the florets, leaving the stems about 1 inch long. Discard the thick stem and leaves. Cut the florets in half lengthwise and then split lengthwise again (and again for large florets) to make ½-inch-thick pieces containing both florets and stems. This method will yield bite-size pieces that cook quickly and evenly.

Lightly oil a skillet with the olive oil and warm it on medium-high heat for about a minute. Remove from the heat, add the cauliflower, salt, and water, cover tightly, and return to high heat. Cook, shaking the skillet now and again, for about 5 minutes until the cauliflower is tender and the water is gone.

Uncover the skillet, turn off the heat, add the Garlic Herb Butter, and allow it to melt. Toss the cauliflower to coat evenly and serve.

Onions au Gratin

SERVES 4

While it's true that onions contain some natural sugars and eating large quantities of them might not be suitable during the earliest stages of a low-carb intervention, they make a tasty accompaniment to a meal. They're a good source of potassium, too. Prepared this way, a cheesy, bubbling hot side dish serving weighs in at only a bit over seven grams of usable carbohydrate. Perfect for transition and maintenance use and an acceptable treat for onion lovers at any time.

Protein per serving:
7.3 grams

Effective carb per serving:
7.2 grams

2 large sweet onions, peeled
1 tablespoon vinegar
2 tablespoons unsalted butter, melted (divided in half for use)
½ cup half-and-half
½ cup freshly grated Parmigiano Reggiano
½ teaspoon salt
½ teaspoon freshly ground black pepper

Preheat the oven to 350 degrees.

Slice the onions into ¼-inch-thick rounds and place into a large bowl; cover with water, add the vinegar, and allow the onions to soak for 15 to 20 minutes. This removes their acrid bite. (If you can get Vidalia or Maui onions, you may omit the soak, as they'll be sweet enough.)

Butter a baking dish with 1 tablespoon of the melted butter.

Drain the onions, pat them dry, and arrange them in a single layer in the baking dish.

In a separate bowl, whisk together the half-and-half, grated cheese, remaining butter, salt, and pepper and pour this mixture over the onions.

Bake for 20 to 30 minutes until bubbling hot and golden. Serve immediately.

CHAPTER 7

◇ ◇ ◇

Condiments, Sauces, and Rubs

◇ ◇ ◇

◇　◇　◇

Adelectable sauce can make a good dish great. What's eggs Benedict, after all, without the Hollandaise? Poached eggs on toast. It's the herbed butter that makes a juicy steakhouse fillet something worthy of its tariff. It's the sweet tanginess of a good barbecue sauce that can elevate a rack of ribs above the pedestrian. It's that little bit of sweet and sour cranberry that snaps the turkey and dressing into focus.

Making a tasty sauce requires nothing more than the crispy brown bits left clinging to the pan after roasting or frying meat, a few aromatic herbs, a bit of something slightly acidic (wine, citrus, vinegar, water, stock) to deglaze the pan, and a little butter, oil, or cream to emulsify it and make it silky. You can use this technique, described in Medallions of Beef Tenderloin with Cabernet Reduction (page 103), to create that mouthwatering little flourish that will set your meat entrees apart from the masses. Feel free to let your creative spirit soar with your choice of aromatics, acids, and oils. For example, try garlic, lemon juice, and butter or olive oil with a last second toss-in of a few capers and voilà, it's piccata. It's that easy.

In this chapter you'll find a simple recipe for our Chicken Pan Gravy and for a pair of famously temperamental sauces—Easy Blender Hollandaise Sauce and Basic Blender Mayonnaise—along with our favorite dry barbecue rub and Spicy Mustard BBQ Sauce. If you're looking for fire, you'll find it in Sesame Fire Butter, a spicy compound butter perfect to top grilled or roasted meat, fish, or poultry or vegetables cooked almost any way. It or its companion, Garlic

Herb Butter, would make a good quick and simple sauce along with a handful of freshly grated Parmigiano Reggiano to toss with low-carb pasta.

Our Simple Tapenade would have fit nicely into chapter 3 with the appetizers, since it's a perfect topping for bruschetta made on low-carb bread, but it's also delicious tossed with pasta, used to coat fish or chicken before baking, or to top them once they're cooked. So we've included it here, with the sauces.

When the holidays roll around, give our fresh Cranberry-Orange Relish a try. It's healthier and much brighter in flavor than the canned or preserved cranberry sauces, and it doesn't take a lot more time than opening the can. We think it will become a repeat performer on your holiday table, as it has on ours. But don't just save it for the turkey—it's great with pork chops, grilled chicken, or duck at any time of the year. Leftover relish, should there be any, would even make a tasty quick addition to Basic Muffins, in chapter 1.

Just a few versatile sauces can turn an ordinary low-carb meal into something memorable and make you feel more like a chef than a short-order cook. All it takes is a little ingenuity—and a few aromatics, some acid, and some oil.

Simple Tapenade

MAKES ABOUT
3 CUPS
(ABOUT 48
TABLESPOONS)

Spread a couple of tablespoons over chicken breasts or fish fillets before baking, spread onto low-carb toast for an appetizer— wherever you use it, the salty, savory flavor of this olive paste will add a gourmet touch to even the simplest dish. It packs a wallop, not only with great taste but also in nutrition from all the good fats and antioxidants it contains.

*Protein per
tablespoon:*
0.2 gram

*Effective carb
per tablespoon:*
0.4 gram

3 cups mixed olives (pitted)
2 anchovy fillets
¼ cup capers
¼ cup oil-packed sun-dried tomatoes
1 cup extra-virgin olive oil

Place the olives into a food processor and pulse to break them up.

Add the anchovies, capers, sun-dried tomatoes, and olive oil and blend until the mixture becomes a chunky paste.

If not using right away, transfer the tapenade to an airtight container and refrigerate for up to a week.

Chicken Pan Gravy

SERVES 4 TO 6

What's fried chicken and mock potatoes without the gravy? Not quite complete, we say. Good pan gravy makes our Spicy Southern Fried Chicken (page 114) and Creamed Fauxtatoes (page 150) seem just like the down-home Sunday suppers of our youth—without the carb load.

Protein per serving:
1.8 grams

Effective carb per serving:
2 grams

2 tablespoons grease from frying chicken*
1 cup chicken stock
2 tablespoons unsalted butter
1 tablespoon almond flour
1 teaspoon ThickenThin not/Starch (see page 9) or 1 teaspoon xanthan gum
½ teaspoon salt
½ teaspoon freshly ground black pepper
1 cup heavy cream

After frying the chicken, pour off all but 2 tablespoons of the fat from the skillet.

Add 2 to 3 tablespoons of chicken stock to deglaze the pan, scraping up all the brown bits.

Now you'll start making an almond flour roux: Add butter to the pan. Sprinkle the almond flour, ThickenThin, salt, and pepper across the pan.

Combine all of the ingredients by pressing and stirring with the tines of a fork.

Add more chicken stock a little at a time, whisking to break up any lumps, until you have a smooth paste. Add the remaining chicken stock, whisking until smooth.

Whisk in the cream and allow the gravy to thicken over medium heat for a few minutes.

*To make gravy without first frying chicken, simply begin with 2 tablespoons of unsalted butter or bacon grease and proceed from there.

Lower-Carb Dry Rub for Meats*

MAKES ABOUT
30 TABLE-
SPOONS

To our way of thinking, a good barbecue spice rub needs to be hot, spicy, and slightly sweet, and this one fills the bill. Feel free to alter the spice or heat to your liking with additions of more of anything except the brown sugar, which would, of course, increase the carbohydrates substantially.

Protein per tablespoon:
0.5 gram

Effective carb per tablespoon:
2.8 grams

½ cup freshly ground black pepper
½ cup paprika
½ cup granular Splenda
2 tablespoons brown sugar
1 tablespoon garlic powder
1 tablespoon onion powder
1 tablespoon cayenne pepper

Place all the ingredients into a ziplock bag and shake to mix.

Store, tightly sealed, in the bag in a cool, dry place. This rub will keep for weeks.

Use by rubbing a few tablespoons onto meats to season prior to barbecuing.

From The 30-Day Low Carb Diet Solution.

Spicy Mustard BBQ Sauce

SERVES 6

We love the sweet and tangy flavor of this easy, quick barbecue sauce. It's perfect for any kind of meat from ribs to brisket to brats and low enough in carb that you can enjoy a healthy quarter-cup serving of it. With more spice than heat, it's mild enough for the tenderfoot; feel free to crank up the heat as far as you like with more cayenne, some habanero sauce, or other hot chile powder for a negligible increase in carbs.

Protein per serving:
0.5 gram

Effective carb per serving:
5.6 grams

1 cup low-carb catsup
¼ onion, grated
1 tablespoon Dijon mustard
½ cup apple cider or red wine vinegar
6 packets Splenda or stevia
1 teaspoon coarse salt
1 teaspoon freshly ground black pepper
1 tablespoon paprika
½ teaspoon onion powder
½ teaspoon garlic powder
1 teaspoon chili powder
¼ teaspoon cayenne pepper (or to taste)

Mix all the ingredients in a saucepan.
   Bring just to a boil over medium heat.
   Reduce the heat and simmer for 15 to 20 minutes.
   Serve hot. The BBQ sauce will keep, tightly sealed, in the refrigerator for up to a week.

Basic Blender Mayonnaise

MAKES ABOUT
1 CUP

Virtually all commercially prepared mayonnaise products are made with partially hydrogenated oil—poor in quality and a recognized health risk. Making your own is a positive step toward better health; it takes only a few minutes and while it's not totally foolproof, it very nearly is. When you discover that homemade mayo is so simple to make and so very good for you, we'll wager that you'll never go back to commercially prepared mayo.

Protein per tablespoon:
0.4 gram

Effective carb per tablespoon:
0.1 gram

1 egg yolk
2 teaspoons champagne vinegar or white wine vinegar
¼ teaspoon salt
½ lemon, juice only (about 1 tablespoon)
dash cayenne pepper (or to taste)
¾ to 1 cup light olive oil or other acceptable oil*

Crack the egg into a blender.

Add the vinegar and salt and blend on low speed. With the motor running, add all remaining ingredients except the oil.

With the motor still running, add the oil in a slow, steady stream until it makes mayonnaise, usually about ¾ to 1 cup. Be careful not to add too much oil or you may break the emulsion and the mayonnaise will separate and clump. Once it reaches the mayonnaise stage, stop adding oil. (Don't despair if your mayonnaise separates and clumps, and don't throw out the result. While it may never thicken to a spreadable form, do save it in a clean container. Up to a week later, you can simply whisk the broken mayo in a bowl with a wire whisk and use it to make mayonnaise-based dressings, which demand a looser emulsion anyway.)

Store in the refrigerator in a clean jar or container with a tight-fitting lid for up to a week.

*Do not use a good extra-virgin olive oil in the blender; for some unknown reason, it can develop a pronounced bitterness. Use light olive oil or any good-quality oil, such as avocado oil, walnut oil, or macadamia oil. For health reasons, we recommend never using any partially hydrogenated oil such as soybean, corn, canola, or vegetable oil, which may contain trans fats.

Easy Blender Hollandaise Sauce*

SERVES 6

If luxury were a sauce, it would be a finely made Hollandaise. One of our most memorable meals occurred years ago at a weekend getaway at the lake home of some dear friends. We dined on whole salmon cooked on the grill and big, juicy asparagus topped with the fluffiest, most delicious Hollandaise we'd ever put in our mouths. Our hostess made it the classic way, in a glass double boiler, the butter whisked in by hand while we talked and drank champagne. This way is easier and almost as good.

Protein per serving:
1.4 grams

Effective carb per serving:
0.5 gram

1 stick (8 tablespoons) unsalted butter
3 egg yolks
2 tablespoons fresh lemon juice
dash cayenne pepper (or to taste)

Melt the butter in a microwave-safe bowl, covered loosely with wax paper.

Meanwhile, in a blender, blend the egg yolks, lemon juice, and cayenne pepper.

With the blender still running, pour the melted butter in a slow stream until it is all incorporated. The sauce should thicken as you blend.

Serve the sauce immediately or hold it for up to 30 minutes over a pan of barely simmering water.

Adapted from The 30-Day Low Carb Diet Solution.

Mexican Cream

MAKES ½ CUP,
APPROXIMATELY
16 GOOD
SQUIRTS

In a past life, we owned a Mexican restaurant and went through gallons of this condiment. While it makes the perfect garnish for enchiladas, quesadillas, and soft tacos, it's equally delicious on omelets, appetizers, soups, and even lasagna. Squirted on with an artistic flourish, it's simple, versatile, tasty, and quick, with better eye appeal than just a dollop.

*Protein per
serving:*
0.2 gram

*Effective carb
per serving:*
0.3 gram

¼ cup sour cream
¼ cup heavy cream or half-and-half

In a small bowl, whisk the creams together until they are completely smooth.

Transfer the mixture to a clean squirt-type dispenser for easy garnishing.

Store, tightly sealed, in the refrigerator for up to a week.

Cranberry-Orange Relish

MAKES ABOUT
24 HEAPING
TABLESPOONS

The bright, fresh zing of this relish will perk up any meal, but we especially enjoy it with holiday meals such as roast turkey or ham, much preferring it to the sugar-filled, jellied cranberry sauces we grew up with. If you love the sweet-tart flavor combination, you're sure to be a fan. Since it's so easy to make and keeps well, you can make it often.

Protein per tablespoon:
0 gram

Effective carb per tablespoon:
2.8 grams

1 whole orange
1½ cups fresh cranberries (about ½ package)
¾ cup granular Splenda

Wash and trim the stem ends from the orange and quarter it. If you prefer, you can zest the orange, peel it, and add only the zest and pulp. You may find that you'll need a bit less sweetener with this alternative method.

Place the quartered orange, including the peel, with the cranberries and Splenda into a food processor fitted with a steel blade.

Pulse to chop the orange and berries to a fine mince.

Taste for sweetness. Depending on the sweetness of the fruit, you may wish to add another 1 to 2 tablespoons of Splenda, although it should taste tangy. Remember that each tablespoon of additional granular Splenda will add 3 grams of carbohydrate to the recipe total.

Turn the mixture into a bowl, cover it tightly with plastic wrap, and refrigerate overnight if possible to develop a more intense flavor.

Serve the relish cold. It will keep, tightly covered, in the refrigerator for up to a week.

Mango Salsa

SERVES 4

When you're in a tropical mood, whip up a batch of this fresh salsa. Its bright color and flavors will perk up everything from Crab Cakes (page 134) to our Shrimp Quesadilla (page 138). It's delicious, too, on grilled fish or chicken.

Protein per serving:
0.5 gram

Effective carb per serving:
6.2 grams

1 large lime, juice and zest
1 packet Splenda or stevia
¼ teaspoon salt
¼ teaspoon freshly ground black pepper
⅛ teaspoon cayenne pepper
⅛ teaspoon ground cumin
3 tablespoons olive oil
1 mango, peeled and diced small
1 red tomato, seeded and diced
4 green onions, chopped
2 tablespoons chopped fresh cilantro

Place the lime juice, zest, sweetener, salt, pepper, and spices into a bowl and allow them to sit for a few minutes.

Whisk in the olive oil completely.

Add all the remaining ingredients and toss to coat evenly.

Serve at room temperature. Refrigerate any leftover salsa for up to a day.

Sesame Fire Butter

**MAKES 8
TABLESPOONS**

If you love hot, spicy foods, you'll want to keep a stick or two of this butter in the freezer to add a bit of savory fire to anything from grilled fish or chicken to roasted, steamed, or stir-fried vegetables.

*Protein per
tablespoon:*
1.2 grams

*Effective carb
per tablespoon:*
0.9 gram

1 stick unsalted butter, softened
1 clove garlic, minced fine or pressed
2 tablespoons toasted sesame seeds
1 tablespoon crushed red pepper flakes
1 teaspoon freshly ground black pepper
2 tablespoons soy sauce

In a food processor, beat the softened butter with the garlic, sesame seeds, and dry spices.

With the motor running, drizzle in the soy sauce, processing until fully incorporated.

Turn the mixture onto a piece of waxed paper and re-form it into a stick. Wrap it securely in the waxed paper and refrigerate it for several hours until firm.

Remove the stick from the refrigerator and cut it into 8 equal pats. Rewrap and place into a ziplock freezer bag. Store frozen for up to 6 weeks. Use individual pats as needed.

Garlic Herb Butter

MAKES 8
TABLESPOONS

A restaurateur friend of ours taught us long ago to keep some herbed butter on hand in the freezer. We add a pat of it to roasted vegetables or melt it onto steaks in their last moments on the grill to add incredible flavor with little effort. This one uses a combination of herbs we like, but feel free to use whatever fresh herbs you enjoy, and even make several types that feature different flavors, for instance, lemon zest and dill for fish, rosemary and sage for pork or poultry, and crushed peppercorn and tarragon for beef.

Protein per tablespoon:
0.2 gram

Effective carb per tablespoon:
0.4 gram

1 stick unsalted butter, softened
2 cloves garlic, minced or pressed
2 tablespoons chopped fresh flat-leaf parsley
1 tablespoon chopped fresh chives
1 tablespoon fresh rosemary leaves
1 tablespoon fresh thyme leaves

Place all the ingredients into a food processor and pulse until well blended.

Turn the mixture onto a piece of waxed paper and re-form it into a stick. Wrap it securely in the waxed paper and refrigerate it for several hours until firm.

Remove the stick from the refrigerator and cut it into 8 equal pats. Rewrap and place into a ziplock freezer bag. Store frozen for up to 6 weeks. Use individual pats as needed.

Thai Peanut Sauce

SERVES 6

We love this slightly hot, slightly sweet, slightly salty sauce as a marinade and condiment for grilled chicken skewers (Chicken Satay page 124), but it's also delicious as a marinade on roasted whole chicken, shrimp, fish, or pork tenders. Try it tossed with steamed spaghetti squash and a handful of toasted sesame seeds as a side dish for Asian-inspired meals.

Protein per serving:
6.7 grams

Effective carb per serving:
3.6 grams

½ cup natural peanut butter
2 packets Splenda or stevia
¼ cup soy sauce
1 tablespoon rice vinegar or white wine vinegar
¼ teaspoon salt
¼ teaspoon freshly ground black pepper
5 or 6 drops of Tabasco (or to taste)
1 tablespoon hot water (approximately)

In a bowl, beat together the peanut butter, sweetener, soy sauce, and vinegar.

Add the salt, pepper, and Tabasco and mix thoroughly. Check the heat and add more hot sauce if desired.

While stirring, dribble in the hot water to thin the sauce to the consistency of unwhipped heavy cream.

CHAPTER 8

◇　◇　◇

Just Desserts

Tender Almond Pie and Tart Crust

All-American Apple Pie

Individual Pumpkin Pies

Creamy Coconut Pie

Rustic Fruit Crostata

Drunken Rubies (Pomegranates in Sweet Red Wine)

Raspberry Coulis

Poached Pears in Sweet Cabernet Reduction Sauce

French Vanilla Ice Cream Deluxe

Bit O' Sweet Glaze

Bittersweet Chocolate Glaze

Classic Chocolate Truffles

Traditional Shortbread Cookies

Handmade Marshmallows

Guiltless Margaritas

Guiltless Mojitos

Traditional Eggnog

Parisian-Style Hot Cho-Co-Late

◇   ◇   ◇

◇　◇　◇

For years, dessert in the low-carb camp meant a bowlful of berries with whipped cream—still a good option and one that we truly enjoy and have often—or sugar-free gelatin or pudding, neither of which we would recommend any longer, since the commercial preparations are almost always sweetened with aspartame. Sadly, the traditional low-carb dessert cart was pretty bare—until recently. As more and more people, including food manufacturers, have hopped aboard the low-carb train, the number of commercially prepared dessert options has taken a strong uptick. Some of the commercial offerings still fall short in palate appeal, but some of the low-carb ice creams, for instance, are quite tasty.

One must always, however, obey the dictum Caveat emptor! (Buyer beware!) with regard to commercially prepared low-carb foods, and nowhere is that more important than with low-carb desserts. It is in the sweet categories that manufacturers tend to play fast and loose with the labeling rules, and many such products that trumpet few or even zero net carbs on their packages contain far more than a small amount—in fact, quite a slug—of such potentially insidious ingredients as glycerin and sugar alcohols. Some manufacturers misunderstand (or, perhaps to be less generous, frankly subvert) our effective carbohydrate concept by adding fiber, glycerin, and/or sugar alcohols to their products and declaring that these substances count as negative carbohydrates, somehow canceling out the starch carbs but not counting as carbs themselves. This truly is fuzzy math, as George W. Bush would say, and even fuzzier thinking. It's another proof of our philosophy that the best thing you can do for yourself is to spend more time in your own kitchen. If you make it yourself, then and often only then will you know what's in it.

All sugars, starches, fibers, polydextrose, maltodextrin, glycerin, and sugar alcohols of any type should be included in the total carbohydrate content on any honest label. After that, the grams of dietary fiber can be removed in their entirety from the carbohydrate gram total and *some portion but not all* of the partially absorbable carbohydrates—polydextrose, maltodextrin, glycerin, and sugar alcohols—can also be deducted to yield the effective (net) carb content. These partially absorbable substances vary widely, not only in their degree and speed of absorption into the bloodstream and hence their contribution to effective carbohydrate grams and calories, but also in their impact on blood sugar and insulin. Our rule of thumb at this point is to count 1 effective (net) gram of carb for every 3 grams of the sugar alcohols or glycerin and about 1 effective gram for every 10 grams of polydextrose used in a recipe. This figure is merely a guesstimate, but it's an educated one. Food scientists and researchers are busily constructing tables to provide this information, but new sugar alcohols seem to be cropping up faster than they can keep up. We'll try to offer this rapidly changing information on our Web sites, www.proteinpower.com and www.lowcarbcookworx.com, as soon as we can.

We've tried to include in this chapter some of what we'd consider our best-loved desserts in a reduced-carb form without sacrificing much in taste, texture, or appearance. You'll find assorted cakes, pies, cookies, puddings, candy, and even some party beverages. All of them are reduced in carb by at least half to two-thirds over the original, some even a bit more; in all cases they represent quite a savings in sugar. Be aware, however, that while these desserts are carb reduced, they're not necessarily calorie reduced, though some contain fewer calories than the original they replace. Consume them sensibly; eat them in moderation, secure in the knowledge that they won't have nearly the impact on your blood sugar or insulin metabolism or promote the degree of weight gain that the "real" thing would. But recognize that these are not "free" foods. Many of them are calorie, protein, and fat rich; if you eat too much of them or eat them too often during your corrective dieting phase, you will surely undermine your weight-loss efforts. Dessert in any sensible lifestyle should always be viewed as a treat, even if, as in this case, a little kitchen alchemy has made it a lower-carb one.

Just as with other baking, creating low-carb versions of cakes, pies, cookies, and pastry dough demands learning to make some simple substitutions for the flour and sugar that form the basis of most sweets. As we discussed in chapter 1, we rely chiefly on almond flour or meal to replace about half of the flour in most of these recipes, with the balance usually made up of combinations of low-carb whey protein, bran, fiber thickeners and bulking agents, and occasionally a little real flour. You will see many similarities from one recipe to the next in these adaptations and quickly catch on to the technique; before long, you'll be an old hand at adapting favorites from your own recipe box. We hope that when you do, you'll share them with your fellow low carbers on our Web sites.

You'll notice that the sugar replacement we most often specify in these recipes is Splenda, either in packets (which are lower in carb) or bulk granular form. This choice has been made for a couple of reasons: Splenda is readily available in regular grocery stores; it holds up well in taste and texture in baking; most people find its taste clean and pleasant; and to date we have seen no credible scientific information that would indict it as a health risk. We do reserve the right to change our minds about its safety (as we did about aspartame years ago) if convincing data comes to light. And if it does, you can be assured you'll hear it from us posthaste.

There are, of course, already those out there who are gunning for Splenda—most notably the sugar producers, who, we think it can be fairly said, have an obvious ax to grind. The current campaign, designed to scare the public away from Splenda, involves a claim that feeding it to your kids is like giving them chlorine. To be sure, the chemical structure of Splenda does contain the chloride ion, but then so does table salt. So far we're unimpressed with the doubters. At this point, Splenda seems to be acceptable: it tastes good, it works well, and it doesn't cause obvious side effects for most people. That's not to say that Splenda is a necessary part of a low-carb diet. In a perfect low-carb world, we would content ourselves with the natural sweetness in foods, but the dessert genie came out of the bottle long ago and most of us can't seem to get her back in there. If you prefer not to use Splenda, feel free to substitute another nonnutritive sweetener, such as stevia powder, xylitol, erythritol, Lo Han Guo, or saccharine as you see fit, recognizing that these recipes may not work in exactly the same way.

In the meantime, we are working hard with food manufacturers and suppliers to find a natural sweetener or combination of them that tastes as good and works as well in recipes as Splenda and doesn't have any unpleasant side effects. We will keep you posted of our progress on our Web sites.

Golden Pound Cake

SERVES 12

Buttery, rich, moist, and delicious, this cake stands alone as a delicious dessert with a cup of steaming coffee, but it also works well as a base for fruit shortcakes and as a substitute for the sponge cake in a trifle or the ladyfingers in Tiramisu (page 198).

Protein per serving:
6 grams

Effective carb per serving:
10.9 grams

1½ cups almond flour
½ cup rice flour
2 tablespoons ThickenThin not/Sugar (see page 9)
1 teaspoon baking powder
pinch salt (or to taste)
1½ sticks (12 tablespoons) unsalted butter, softened
1 cup granular Splenda
5 eggs, separated
2 teaspoons vanilla extract

Preheat the oven to 350 degrees.

Butter two small loaf pans and line the bottoms with parchment. Butter the parchment, too.

Combine all the dry ingredients except the Splenda.

In a separate bowl, beat the softened butter until fluffy, beat in half the Splenda until blended, then beat in the remainder. Beat in the egg yolks one at a time. Add the vanilla and stir until blended. Do not overbeat.

Add the dry ingredients by hand and stir until combined, but do not beat. The batter will be quite stiff and heavy.

Beat the egg whites until they hold soft peaks and gently but thoroughly fold them into the batter.

Turn the batter into the loaf pans.

Bake for about 40 minutes until a toothpick inserted into the center comes out clean.

Cool the loaf pans on a rack briefly. Remove the loaves from the pan and cool fully on a rack before slicing.

Luscious Yellow Layer Cake

For birthdays, anniversaries, or bon voyage gatherings, it just isn't a party without the cake. This one looks, feels, and tastes almost as good as the high-carb original, but it won't leave you with a morning-after carb hangover. Note that it's not ultra low carb—it still has almost 12 grams of effective carb per serving before frosting—and as such, it is a treat best saved for maintenance, enjoyed sparingly, or split with a friend during correction.

Protein per serving:
5.5 grams

Effective carb per serving:
11.4 grams

½ cup cake flour

1 cup almond flour

½ cup rice bran

2 tablespoons ThickenThin not/Sugar (see page 9)

2½ teaspoons baking powder

¼ teaspoon fine salt

10 tablespoons unsalted butter, room temperature

¾ cup granular Splenda

15 packets Splenda

4 eggs

1 teaspoon pure vanilla extract

¼ teaspoon almond extract

¾ cup half-and-half

Preheat the oven to 350 degrees.

Generously butter the bottom and sides of two 9-inch cake pans; cover the bottom of the pans with parchment paper, butter the parchment, then dust each pan with about 1 tablespoon of ThickenThin. Invert to remove any excess and set aside.

In a mixing bowl, combine all the dry ingredients except the Splenda.

In a separate bowl, cream the butter with an electric mixer until smooth, then add all the Splenda. Continue beating until the mixture is light, about 3 minutes.

Beat in the eggs one at a time, add the vanilla and almond extracts, and beat another few seconds to mix.

Add ⅓ of the dry ingredients to the butter and egg mixture and beat just until incorporated, then add ⅓ of the half-and-half and beat briefly. Alternate the dry and half-and-half additions until all the ingredients are incorporated. Do not overbeat or the cake will be tough.

Scrape the mixture evenly into the cake pans and bake for about 25 minutes. A toothpick inserted into the center should come out clean.

Cool the pans for 5 minutes on a rack, then remove the cakes from the pans by inverting them onto the rack. Cool completely.

Top with Cream Cheese Frosting (page 192), Vanilla Buttercream Frosting (page 193), or your favorite low-carb frosting.

VARIATION

Low-Carb Yellow Cupcakes. Make the batter as above. Generously butter two 12-cup muffin tins and line them with cupcake papers. Fill each cup nearly full and bake them at 350 degrees for 20 to 25 minutes. Cool the cupcakes completely, then frost them with your choice of low-carb frosting.

Coconut-Almond Cake

SERVES 12

Here's the perfect cake for springtime holiday celebrations. If you're a fan of coconut, you will love this dense, sweet, and very rich cake. This recipe is not ultra low in carb or low in calories, but it is suitable for a special occasion without causing metabolic mayhem. This cake is filling; a thin slice will go a long way. It contains only a fraction of the nearly 60 grams of carb of the original but retains its moist texture and delicious coconut-almond flavor combination.

Protein per serving:
15 grams

Effective carb per serving:
11 grams

6 tablespoons unsalted butter, room temperature
½ cup granular Splenda
24 packets Splenda
2 teaspoons almond extract
2 tablespoons ThickenThin not/Sugar (see page 9)
6 large eggs
½ cup unsweetened coconut milk
½ teaspoon coconut extract
1½ cups almond flour
¼ cup cake flour
¼ cup low-carb whey protein powder, vanilla or natural flavor
2 teaspoons baking powder
¼ teaspoon salt
1 cup shredded or flaked unsweetened coconut

FROSTING
1½ cups heavy cream
3 packets Splenda or stevia

Preheat the oven to 325 degrees.

Generously grease a 9-inch springform pan with coconut oil and dust it with a bit of almond meal.

In a bowl, with an electric mixer, cream the butter and then beat in all the Splenda, the almond extract, and ThickenThin. Add the eggs one at a time and beat between each addition. Add the coconut milk and mix briefly.

Add the coconut extract and beat the mixture on high for a couple of minutes.

In a separate bowl, combine the almond flour, cake flour, protein powder, baking powder, and salt. Add about ½ the coconut flakes and mix well.

Add the dry mixture to the wet ingredients and mix just to combine. Do not overbeat.

Pour the batter into the prepared pan and bake for 45 to 50 minutes until a toothpick inserted into the center comes out clean.

Cool the cake in the pan for 10 minutes, then remove the spring-form ring. Cool the cake completely before frosting.

Whip the heavy cream and 2 packets of the sweetener until firm peaks form and frost the entire cake. Toss the remaining coconut with 1 packet of sweetener and sprinkle over the top of the cake.

Flourless Chocolate Cake

SERVES 12

This intensely chocolate treat finds its way to the dessert carts of many upscale restaurants, variously called Molten Chocolate Cake and Baked Fudge. Those monikers give you a glimpse into its dark, delicious nature. Flourless sounds low carb, but traditionally prepared, these cakes contain the equivalent of about a cup of sugar in the bittersweet or semisweet chocolate usually used. This one, however, doesn't bring the heavy dose of sugar with it, just the decadent taste.

Protein per serving:
9.8 grams

Effective carb per serving:
9.5 grams

8 eggs
1 cup granular Splenda*
1 pound unsweetened chocolate, coarsely chopped
2 sticks (16 tablespoons) unsalted butter
¼ cup strong coffee or espresso

Preheat the oven to 325 degrees.

Line the bottom of an 8-inch springform pan with parchment and generously butter the sides. Wrap the bottom and sides of the pan with a single sheet of heavy-duty aluminum foil to make it waterproof. Set the springform pan in a roasting pan that you will subsequently fill with boiling water.

Place the eggs into a mixing bowl and beat with an electric mixer on high speed for about 5 minutes until their volume doubles. Beat in the sweetener.

In a large heatproof mixing bowl set over a pan of barely simmering water, put the chocolate, butter, and coffee and stir frequently until the mixture becomes smooth.

Fold about ⅓ of the egg foam into the chocolate mixture. When just a few streaks of egg remain visible, fold in half of the remaining

*You may substitute 24 packets of Splenda or stevia plus 1 tablespoon of ThickenThin not/Sugar or 1 cup of granular xylitol or erythritol for the sweetener. You can even add a bit more sweetener (6 to 8 additional packets) if you don't mind a tiny increase in carb per serving.

egg foam in the same manner. Finally, fold the remaining portion of the egg foam until all of it is completely incorporated.

Scrape the batter into the prepared springform pan and smooth the surface with a spatula.

Set the roasting pan into the oven and carefully pour boiling water to come halfway up the sides of the foil-wrapped springform pan.

Bake for 22 to 25 minutes until an instant thermometer inserted into the center reads 140 degrees or until the sides pull away slightly and a thin, shiny, brownielike crust has formed on the surface.

When cooked, remove the springform pan from the water bath and cool on a wire rack to room temperature. Cover and refrigerate the cake overnight or up to several (3 to 4) days.

When ready to serve, remove the springform sides, invert the cake onto waxed paper, remove the parchment liner from the bottom, and invert the cake again onto a serving plate.

Garnish each slice with a dollop of sweetened whipped cream, and plate each slice on a pool of Raspberry Coulis (page 215) or drizzle the plate with a tablespoon of Sweet Cabernet Reduction Sauce (page 216), the latter two of which will add some carbs, so be sure to count them.

Darned Good Carrot Cake

SERVES 12

Okay, nobody makes a carrot cake quite like Mom, but this one really is darned good. It comes pretty close to capturing the dense moistness and flavor of the original but does so with a fraction of the carb load, making it something we can indulge in more often.

Protein per serving:
11 grams:
9.3 grams (cake),
1.7 grams
(frosting)

Effective carb per serving:
15.9 grams:
10.7 grams (cake),
5.2 grams
(frosting)

4 eggs

1 cup liquid coconut oil

1¼ cups almond flour

½ cup oat bran

¼ cup whole-wheat flour

4 tablespoons ThickenThin not/Sugar (see page 9) or
    1 tablespoon xanthan gum

36 packets Splenda

1 teaspoon salt

2 teaspoons baking powder

2 teaspoons baking soda

2 teaspoons cinnamon

3 cups grated carrots

1 cup chopped pecans

⅛ teaspoon nutmeg

Preheat the oven to 350 degrees.

Lightly butter two 9 × 9-inch cake pans and line the bottoms with parchment. Lightly butter the parchment.

In a large bowl, beat the eggs and beat in the oil.

In a separate bowl, mix the dry ingredients well.

Add the dry ingredients to the wet ingredients and mix thoroughly but do not overbeat.

Fold in the grated carrots and pecans by hand, distributing them evenly throughout the mixture. The batter will be quite heavy.

Divide the batter between the two pans.

Bake for 25 to 30 minutes until the cake springs back slightly to the touch. Do not overcook.

Cool thoroughly on wire racks before frosting.

TO FROST

Prepare one recipe Cream Cheese Frosting (page 192).

Spread one-half of the frosting on the bottom layer, leaving the sides bare. Top with the second layer and spread the remaining frosting on top, leaving the sides bare.

Sprinkle the chopped pecans across the top.

Cream Cheese Frosting

SERVES 12

What's a carrot cake or a spice cake without a cream cheese frosting? Incomplete! This one is easy on the carb load but retains all the creamy sweetness of the original. It makes a great filling or frosting for cupcakes or brownies as well. To use as a filling, simply pipe the frosting from a pastry bag directly into the center of a warm cupcake with a large piping tip.

Protein per serving:
1.7 grams

Effective carb per serving:
5.9 grams

8 ounces cream cheese, softened
1 stick unsalted butter, softened
1 cup granular Splenda
12 packets Splenda
2 tablespoons ThickenThin not/Sugar (see page 9) or
    2 teaspoons xanthan gum
2 teaspoons vanilla extract
¼ cup finely chopped pecans

Beat the cream cheese and butter until fluffy and smooth.
    Beat in the Splenda, ThickenThin, and vanilla.
    By hand, fold in the pecans.

Vanilla Buttercream Frosting

Lighter on the carbs, but full of the traditional fluffy, sweet taste you love, this frosting will dress up cakes, cupcakes, and even brownies. You can not only can you tint it with cake decorating colors to make a rainbow of frosting shades, you can flavor it as you choose with lemon, orange, peppermint, butterscotch, maple, almond, or even coffee in place of the vanilla for a range of tasty buttercream variations. This recipe makes enough to frost one 9-inch layer cake or 24 cupcakes.

Protein per serving:
0.2 gram (for 12),
0.1 gram (for 24)

Effective carb per serving:
13 grams (for 12),
6.5 grams (for 24)

1 stick (8 tablespoons) unsalted butter, softened

3 cups granular Splenda

12 packets Splenda or stevia

3 tablespoons ThickenThin not/Sugar (see page 9) or
    2 teaspoons xanthan gum

6 tablespoons heavy cream

2 tablespoons vanilla extract

In a mixing bowl, cream the butter with an electric mixer.

Add the sweeteners and ThickenThin little by little, alternating with a few tablespoons of cream, beating well after each addition.

Add the vanilla and stir to combine.

If the frosting is too thick, add an additional teaspoon or two of cream. Refrigerate for a few minutes if too thin.

Chocolate Buttercream Frosting

SERVES 12 TO 24

When you're a chocolate junkie, nothing but the most intense and rich chocolate frosting will do. This one is sure to please even the most dedicated fan. This recipe makes enough to frost one 9-inch layer cake (about 12 servings) or 24 cupcakes.

Protein per serving:
0.8 gram (for 12),
0.4 gram (for 24)

Effective carb per serving:
11 grams (for 12),
5.5 grams (for 24)

2 ounces premium unsweetened baking chocolate, finely chopped
1 stick (8 tablespoons) unsalted butter, softened
2 cups granular Splenda
25 packets Splenda or stevia
3 tablespoons ThickenThin not/Sugar (see page 9)
6 tablespoons heavy cream
2 tablespoons vanilla extract

In a heatproof mixing bowl over a pan of barely simmering water, melt the chocolate, stirring frequently, and when smooth, remove from the heat.

In a separate mixing bowl, cream the butter with an electric mixer.

Add the Splenda little by little, alternating with a few tablespoons of cream, beating well after each addition.

When you have added about half the Splenda, scrape the melted chocolate into the frosting and mix well. Add the ThickenThin, remaining sweetener, and cream. Beat the mixture until it is completely smooth.

Add the vanilla and stir to combine.

If the frosting is too thick, add an additional teaspoon or two of cream. Refrigerate for a few minutes if too thin.

Scrumptious Shortcakes

SERVES 12

Summer parties at our house, particularly on the Fourth of July, usually call for strawberry or peach shortcake. In years gone by, that meant a pile of fruit and syrup over homemade biscuits, but the carb counts made having that treat a rare occurrence. These shortcakes retain the buttery, crumbly goodness of the originals, and we can have them much more often.

Protein per serving:
3 grams

Effective carb per serving:
5.8 grams

2 cups almond flour
½ cup whole-wheat flour
½ cup oat bran
1 tablespoon baking powder
¼ teaspoon salt
10 tablespoons unsalted butter, cold
½ cup heavy cream
3 large egg yolks
1 teaspoon pure vanilla extract

Preheat the oven to 425 degrees.

Combine all the dry ingredients in a large mixing bowl.

Cut the butter into small cubes.

Working quickly, cut the butter into the dry mixture with a fork or your fingertips until it reaches the consistency of coarse meal with a few butter pebbles remaining.

In a small bowl, lightly beat the cream with the egg yolks and vanilla.

Make a well in the center of the dry ingredients.

Pour the cream mixture into the well and with a fork, gently bring the dry ingredients into the wet until just combined. Do not overmix or the cakes will be tough.

Turn out onto a board dusted with a bit of almond flour and sprinkle a bit more almond flour on top of the wet dough.

Very gently knead the dough by folding over and flattening slightly just a couple of times. Again, do not overdo it or the cakes will be tough.

Gently flatten the dough into a circle about ¾ inch thick.

Cut across the diameter, as you would a pie, to make 6 triangles, then cut each triangle in half.

Place the cakes onto a parchment-lined or buttered baking sheet and bake for 20 to 25 minutes.

Cool the cakes completely. To serve, split each cake and top with fresh low-carb strawberry, blueberry, blackberry, or peach shortcake filling and a dollop of whipped cream.

Strawberry Shortcake Filling

SERVES 8

Although strawberries can be had in grocery stores almost all year, we think it best to save this delectable treat for strawberry season, when the berries come ripe straight from the vines, bursting with flavor. Artificial sweeteners don't draw the juices from the berries as sugar does, but you can make a pretty good syrup using a little ThickenThin not/Sugar as we've done here. Just as with the original, let the berries macerate overnight in the refrigerator if you have the time.

Protein per serving:
0.5 gram

Effective carb per serving:
8.5 grams

½ cup granular Splenda*
1 cup water
1 tablespoon ThickenThin not/Sugar (see page 9)
2 pints fresh strawberries

MAKE A LOW-CARB SIMPLE SYRUP

In a small saucepan, dissolve the Splenda in the water.

Add the ThickenThin, sprinkling in and whisking to avoid lumps.

In a small bowl, mash 2 or 3 of the ripest strawberries and add to the syrup.

Heat the syrup gently for a few minutes and set aside to thicken slightly.

Wash, stem, and quarter the strawberries and place into a bowl.

Pour the syrup over the berries, cover, and refrigerate for 2 to 3 hours or overnight.

*You can save even more grams of carbohydrate by using 12 packets of Splenda or stevia in place of the ½ cup of granular Splenda.

Tiramisu

SERVES 10

If you love this rich and decadent classic Italian dessert, this is the recipe for you. There are no sacrifices here in taste, texture, or satisfaction. Although it contains only a fraction of the carb per serving of the original version, it's clearly not ultra low in carb or calories, so eat sparingly and enjoy fully. The recipe may appear a bit daunting, but don't fret; you can make the pound cake and espresso syrup even several days ahead, then only have to deal with the Mascarpone filling and assembly, which goes pretty fast.

Protein per serving:
10.6 grams

Effective carb per serving:
20 grams
(This dessert is best reserved for maintenance, when a 20-gram splurge now and then isn't going to make much of an impact. During the weight-loss or corrective phases of a low-carb diet, enjoy just a half piece as an *occasional* treat.)

1 loaf Golden Pound Cake (page 183)
1 recipe Espresso Syrup
1 recipe Mascarpone Filling

ESPRESSO SYRUP
½ cup strong brewed espresso
⅓ cup Splenda
⅓ cup brandy

MASCARPONE FILLING
4 large egg yolks
⅓ cup Splenda
¼ cup dry marsala wine
½ pound mascarpone cheese, softened
½ pound cream cheese, softened

TO MAKE THE SYRUP
Stir the Splenda into the hot espresso to dissolve.
   Add the brandy.
   Set aside to cool.

TO MAKE THE FILLING
Whisk the egg yolks, Splenda, and marsala wine in a bowl.
   Whisk the egg yolk mixture over a pan of simmering water for 2 to 3 minutes until foamy and thickening.
   Remove the yolks from the heat.

With an electric mixer, whip the mixture on medium speed until cooled.

Beat in the mascarpone and cream cheeses.

TO ASSEMBLE

Cut the Golden Pound Cake in half across the middle and down the length to make four quarters. Cut each quarter into three thin slices lengthwise.

Line the bottom of a 2-quart gratin dish or a glass loaf or baking dish with four slices of the cake.

Soak the cakes with ⅓ of the espresso syrup.

Spread the cakes with ⅓ of the mascarpone filling.

Top with four more cake slices, soak them with another ⅓ of the syrup, and add another ⅓ of the mascarpone filling.

Finish with another layer of cake, soaked with espresso syrup and topped with mascarpone filling.

Dust the cakes with unsweetened cocoa powder.

Cover and refrigerate for several hours before serving.

Decadent Espresso Chocolate Mousse

SERVES 6

Rich and chocolaty, dense and airy at the same time, slightly bittersweet—all these terms fail to adequately describe the character of this bit of culinary decadence. Sure, it takes a little bit of prep ahead of time, but the result is worth the small effort. As new research points to the heart-healthy qualities of good chocolate, it's decadence you can feel good about. We love to serve it in tiny ramekins, enough to give dinner guests just a taste. In that case, you can easily make 12 servings with this recipe.

Protein per serving:
5.7 grams

Effective carb per serving:
7.1 grams

17 packets Splenda (divided for use)
⅔ cup heavy cream plus ⅓ cup heavy cream (divided for use)
4 ounces unsweetened premium chocolate, finely and evenly chopped
1¼ teaspoons plus ¼ teaspoon instant espresso powder (divided for use)
1 tablespoon coffee liqueur (such as Kahlúa)
2 eggs
1 tablespoon water
½ teaspoon pure vanilla extract

In a large heatproof mixing bowl, stir 12 packets of Splenda into ⅓ cup of the cream.

Create a double boiler by placing the bowl over a saucepan of simmering water and add the chocolate pieces and ¼ teaspoon of espresso powder. Stir frequently as the chocolate melts until it is completely smooth.

Remove the bowl from the heat and stir in the coffee liqueur.

In a separate medium heatproof mixing bowl, whisk the eggs, 3 packets of Splenda, and the water until well blended.

Place this bowl atop the pan of barely simmering water and whisk constantly until the egg mixture thickens somewhat (ideally, until it reaches 160 degrees on an instant thermometer).

Remove the bowl from the heat and beat at high speed with an electric mixer for 3 or 4 minutes until the mixture attains the consistency of soft whipped cream. Stir in the vanilla.

Fold ¼ of the egg mixture into the melted chocolate. Scrape in the remaining egg mixture, gently folding until the egg is just evenly incorporated. Don't overmix or you will lose the light moussiness of the finished product.

Divide the mixture evenly among 6 ramekins and chill for at least one hour.

Before serving, whip the remaining cream with the final 2 packets of Splenda and the remaining espresso powder until nearly stiff.

To serve, top each mousse with a dollop of sweet espresso cream.

Crème Brûlée*

SERVES 4 TO 6

This signature dining-out indulgence is quicker and easier to make than you might ever have imagined. We prefer it pure, but feel free to let your imagination run free in adding other flavors: as you warm it, infuse the cream with lavender, orange peel, or ginger. (Strain the cream before proceeding.) Or try dissolving a tablespoon each of espresso powder, unsweetened chocolate powder, and Splenda into the cream if mocha is your thing—it's your indulgence, after all!

Protein per serving:
3.9 grams

Effective carb per serving:
3.3 grams

1½ cups heavy cream or half-and-half
½ cup water
10 packets Splenda
2 teaspoons pure vanilla extract
salt (to taste)
4 egg yolks

Preheat the oven to 300 degrees.

Generously butter 4 to 6 shallow ovenproof ramekins and set them in a shallow baking pan.

Put all the ingredients except the egg yolks into a saucepan over medium-low heat and warm the cream, stirring often. Do not let the cream boil.

In a separate bowl (or a 4-cup glass measuring cup), beat the egg yolks until they are smooth and pale.

When the cream is hot and sending up a little steam, temper the eggs with it by dribbling a tablespoon or two of the cream into the yolks, whisking constantly to prevent the egg yolks from cooking. Repeat the tempering once or twice and then pour in the remainder of the hot cream, whisking constantly.

Divide the cream mixture evenly among the buttered ramekins and place them into the oven. Fill the baking pan with hot water to reach approximately halfway up the ramekins.

From The Low-Carb Comfort Food Cookbook.

Bake the custard for about 30 minutes. It should be pale and shake like jelly when you tap the ramekin.

Remove the custard from the oven; when cool, cover the ramekins and refrigerate.

When ready to serve, remove from the refrigerator 10 or 15 minutes ahead and top each custard with 1 teaspoon of brown or granulated sugar. Caramelize the sugar either under the broiler for $1\frac{1}{2}$ to 2 minutes or with a kitchen torch* to form the crisp caramel top crust.

*The kitchen torch is a small butane (or propane) torch available at most kitchen specialty stores or online. It is used to put quick high heat to food to caramelize the outside or top.

Chewy Fudge Brownies

SERVES 16

These brownies will satisfy your chocolate craving without much of a dent in your carb budget. They're so deeply chocolaty and rich that one or two is all you'll need to finish off a meal. We love them with a little low-carb ice cream as Ice Cream Browniewiches (page 205) for a summertime treat.

Protein per serving:
1.9 grams

Effective carb per serving:
1.8 grams

1 stick unsalted butter
2 ounces unsweetened baking chocolate, roughly chopped
24 packets Splenda
2 eggs
½ teaspoon vanilla extract
⅛ teaspoon salt
½ cup almond flour
1 tablespoon ThickenThin not/Sugar (see page 9)

Preheat the oven to 350 degrees.

In a medium to large glass mixing bowl, melt the butter in the microwave, about 2 minutes on high. Cover to prevent spattering.

In a medium saucepan, bring about 2 inches of water to a boil and reduce the heat to a simmer to create a double boiler to melt the chocolate.

Add the chopped chocolate to the bowl with the melted butter and place the bowl atop the simmering water in the saucepan. Allow the chocolate to melt.

Remove from the heat, add the Splenda, and stir until the mixture is smooth.

Beat in the eggs one at a time, then beat in the vanilla and salt.

Gently stir in the almond flour and ThickenThin.

Pour the batter into a prepared pan and bake until just set in the middle, 20 to 25 minutes.

Cool the brownies on a rack for 10 to 15 minutes.

Cut the brownies into 16 pieces; store, tightly covered, at room temperature. These brownies will not keep longer than a day or two unless frozen.

Ice Cream Browniewiches

SERVES 6

Grown-ups and kids alike will love these cool, chocolaty ice cream sandwich treats as a dessert or as an afternoon snack. But beware, they'll go fast, so make a triple batch to save time. We like them made with vanilla ice cream, the traditional way, but they're delicious made with everything from strawberry to mint chip to butter pecan.

Protein per serving:
8.5 grams

Effective carb per serving:
10.5 grams

1 recipe Chewy Fudge Brownies (page 204), uncut
2 cups vanilla bean low-carb ice cream, commercial or homemade

Soften the ice cream for 10 to 15 seconds on high in the microwave. If necessary, repeat in 5- to 10-second intervals until it is soft enough to easily handle but not soupy.

Tear a rectangle of heavy aluminum foil and one of plastic wrap each about 18 inches long. Lay the foil down first and put the plastic wrap on top of it.

Cut the 8-inch brownie cake evenly in half and center one half on top of the plastic wrap.

Top the cake half with 2 cups of slightly softened ice cream, spreading it evenly across the brownie cake.

Place the other brownie cake half atop the ice cream and press down gently, firmly, and evenly. Use a spatula to make the edges smooth, if necessary.

Fold the plastic wrap around the cake, then fold the aluminum foil and tightly seal. Place the browniewich cake into the freezer for 15 to 20 minutes to allow the ice cream to become firmer.

Remove the cake, unwrap, and cut the dessert in half, lengthwise, and then each half into thirds to make 6 servings.

If frozen hard, allow the browniewiches to soften slightly before serving. Top with a dollop of whipped cream, if desired.

To save for individual treats, wrap single servings in plastic freezer wrap, place into ziplock freezer bags, and freeze for up to 2 weeks.

Simple Nut Crust

SERVES 8

This delicious crust is perfect for any recipe in which you would have used graham crackers or cookie crumbs; for instance, we use it for cheesecakes or custard tarts. The finer you grind the nuts, the more like cookie crumbs they will seem, but don't take it too far. There's a thin line between fine nut meal and nut butter.

Protein per serving:
5.2 grams

Effective carb per serving:
2.8 grams

1 cup pecan pieces
1 cup walnut pieces
2 tablespoons unsalted butter, melted
¼ cup granular Splenda
pinch fine salt (or to taste)

Preheat the oven to 325 degrees.
    Place all the ingredients into a blender or a food processor.
    Pulse the mixture to a coarse meal.
    Turn the mixture out into a pie pan or divide evenly among 8 individual small custard cups.
    Press the mixture into the bottom and slightly up the sides of the container to form a bottom crust.
    Bake for 5 or 6 minutes, just to set the crust.
    Remove and cool slightly before filling.

Tender Almond Pie and Tart Crust

SERVES 6

Delicate and short, just like Grandma's, this pie and tart crust is not only low in carb but nutritious as well, thanks to the almond meal and whey it contains. It's perfect for traditional one-crust pies, rustic tarts, or savories, such as Chicken Potpie (page 122). For a pie that requires a top crust, you'll need to double the recipe—and remember that doubles the number of carbs the crust will contribute toward your total carb count.

Protein per serving:
7 grams

Effective carb per serving:
2.6 grams

½ cup almond flour
2 tablespoons vital wheat gluten
1 tablespoon ThickenThin not/Sugar (see page 9) or
    1 teaspoon xanthan gum
1 tablespoon natural-flavor whey protein powder
½ teaspoon baking powder
pinch salt (to taste)
2 tablespoons unsalted butter, cold
1 egg yolk
1 to 2 tablespoons water, chilled

Combine the dry ingredients in a medium-size mixing bowl.

Cut in the butter with your fingers, a fork, or a pastry knife until the flour resembles coarse meal.

In a separate small bowl, beat the egg yolk with 1 tablespoon of the water and add these to the dry ingredients, bringing the mixture together with a fork. If it's too dry, add more water by the teaspoonful until just moist.

Bring the dough together in a ball by hand, and if possible, wrap in plastic and chill for 15 to 20 minutes before proceeding. This will make the dough easier to handle.

When ready to bake the pie or tart, roll the chilled dough between sheets of waxed paper or plastic to the desired thickness and diameter required for the specific pie or tart recipe.

All-American Apple Pie

SERVES 8

Whether it's for the Fourth of July, the first crisp autumn day, or a Christmas feast, nothing says American tradition quite like a freshly baked apple pie. This one lets you savor all the tangy sweet taste you love with many fewer carbs, even leaving, at least in maintenance, enough room for a scoop of low-carb vanilla ice cream.

Protein per serving:
10.6 grams

Effective carb per serving:
17.9 grams (Although this number of carbs is workable in maintenance, in the corrective phases of low-carb dieting it would be a splurge not to be enjoyed too often. During the early phases, split a slice with a friend.)

2 recipes Tender Almond Pie and Tart Crusts (page 207)
8 small (or 6 medium) Granny Smith or other tart pie apples
1 lemon, juice only
8 to 10 packets Splenda
2 teaspoons cinnamon
pinch fine salt (or to taste)
1 tablespoon ThickenThin not/Sugar (see page 9) or
    1½ teaspoons xanthan gum
1 tablespoon unsalted butter
1 egg yolk, beaten with 1 tablespoon water

Preheat the oven to 325 degrees.

Prepare two Tender Almond Pie and Tart Crusts. Line a pie plate with one crust. Flute the edge to your liking. Reserve the other for the top crust.

Wash, peel, and slice the apples; place them into a bowl.

Toss the slices with the lemon juice to prevent browning.

In a separate bowl, mix the Splenda, cinnamon, salt, and Thicken-Thin.

Sprinkle the Splenda mixture evenly over the apple slices and toss to coat.

Mound the apple slices into the crust-lined pie pan.

Dot the apples with butter.

Cover the pie with the second crust. Cut 2 or 3 steam vents in the crust.

Brush the egg and water mixture across the top crust to promote browning. Use a piecrust shield or an aluminum foil skirt to protect the fluted edge from burning, if desired.

Bake for about 40 minutes until the apples are soft and the top crust is golden brown.

Individual Pumpkin Pies

SERVES 8

At our house, no Thanksgiving feast would be complete without a pumpkin pie. Because pumpkin itself is naturally low in carb, it doesn't present the problem; it's the wheat crust and the sugar or corn syrup in traditional recipes that wreaks all the metabolic havoc. These individual pies grant automatic portion control, but the custard will also work for a single large pie made with Tender Almond Pie and Tart Crust (page 207) for a more traditional presentation.

Protein per serving:
9.5 grams

Effective carb per serving:
8 grams

1 recipe Simple Nut Crust (page 206)
3 eggs
¾ cup granular Splenda
½ teaspoon ground allspice
⅛ teaspoon freshly grated nutmeg
½ teaspoon ground cinnamon
pinch fine salt (or to taste)
1½ cups canned pumpkin
1½ cups half-and-half

GARNISH
½ cup heavy cream
1 tablespoon ground cinnamon plus 1 tablespoon granular Splenda or
    2 packets stevia

Bake the Simple Nut Crust recipe in 8 individual small custard cups; use the crusts while still warm.

Increase the oven temperature to 375 degrees.

In a saucepan, beat the eggs with the Splenda. Add the spices and salt and stir to mix.

Stir in the canned pumpkin and half-and-half.

Warm the mixture over medium-low heat until hot, but do not boil.

Evenly divide the pumpkin mixture among the 8 custard cups.

Place the filled cups onto a baking sheet and bake for 30 minutes until the cooked filling is moist and quivers when tapped.

Cool the custard cups on a rack.

Serve the individual pies with a dollop of whipped cream and a dusting of cinnamon-Splenda.

Creamy Coconut Pie

SERVES 6

This melt-in-your-mouth pie is every bit as satisfying as the original, much lower in carb, and made even more flavorful with the addition of coconut milk. Packed with protein and good fats, it's a dessert you can actually feel good about indulging in.

Protein per serving:
13.6 grams

Effective carb per serving:
12 grams

¾ cup unsweetened shredded coconut
4 packets Splenda or stevia (divided for use)
1 recipe Tender Almond Pie and Tart Crust (page 207)
¾ cup granular Splenda
1 tablespoon ThickenThin not/Sugar (see page 9)
⅛ teaspoon salt
4 eggs, separated
1 can (14 ounces) premium unsweetened coconut milk
½ cup heavy cream
2 tablespoons unsalted butter, softened
2 teaspoons vanilla extract
⅛ teaspoon cream of tartar

Preheat the oven to 325 degrees.

Toss the coconut with 2 packets of sweetener and lightly toast it in a skillet over very low heat. Shake almost constantly until the coconut just begins to brown. Remove from the heat and set aside.

Prepare the piecrust, pierce the bottom with a fork, and bake it for 10 minutes while you prepare the filling.

When the piecrusts are done, increase the oven temperature to 350 degrees.

In a saucepan, mix the granular Splenda, ThickenThin, and salt.

In a separate bowl, beat together the egg yolks, coconut milk, and cream.

Stir the coconut milk–egg mixture into the dry ingredients in the saucepan, whisking to remove all lumps. Cook the mixture for about 10 minutes over medium heat, stirring constantly as the mixture comes to a boil and thickens.

Remove from the heat and stir in the butter, vanilla extract, and ½ of the toasted coconut.

Using an electric mixer, beat the egg whites with a pinch of salt and the cream of tarter until foamy. Add the remaining packets of sweetener, one by one, and continue to beat until stiff peaks form.

Pour the warm filling into the baked piecrust, top with the meringue, sprinkle the top with the remaining toasted coconut, and bake for 10 to 15 minutes until the meringue is faintly brown.

Allow the pie to cool completely on a rack before serving. Refrigerate to chill, if desired. Store any leftover pie in the refrigerator.

Rustic Fruit Crostata

SERVES 6

The Italian crostata *is nothing more than a free-form tart in which the crust is casually folded back over the fruit filling to leave it partly in view. We entertain often with this simple yet elegant dessert, varying the fruit based on what looks good or what we happen to have on hand. In season, it's often apricots, since we have a prolific tree in our courtyard in Santa Fe.*

Protein per serving:
7.5 grams

Effective carb per serving:
7.8 grams

1 recipe Tender Almond Pie and Tart Crust (page 207)
1 tablespoon unsalted butter
2 cups fresh fruit (sliced peaches or apples or apricot or cherry halves)*
6 packets Splenda
¼ teaspoon cinnamon
pinch salt (or to taste)

GARNISH
½ cup heavy cream
2 packets Splenda or stevia

Preheat the oven to 350 degrees.

Prepare one Tender Almond Pie and Tart Crust and, between two sheets of waxed paper or plastic, roll it into a rough circle about ⅛ inch thick and 10 to 12 inches in diameter. Refrigerate the crust until ready to use.

Melt the butter in a skillet over medium heat.

In a mixing bowl, sprinkle the Splenda, cinnamon, and salt over the sliced fruit and toss to coat evenly.

Sauté the fruit briefly in the butter to soften slightly.

Remove the crust from the refrigerator and center it on a lightly greased baking sheet.

Arrange the fruit slices in a circle, working outward from the center of the pie crust, leaving a margin of about 2 inches all around the outer edge uncovered.

*Fresh berries such as raspberries, blackberries, or blueberries work well also but do not need the sauté step to soften them. Simply arrange the washed and dried berries on the prepared crust, dot with a little butter, sprinkle with Splenda, and bake as directed.

Carefully fold this outer edge up and over the outer couple of inches of the fruit, leaving the edges scalloped and ragged and folding the dough as needed to contain the fruit. Alternatively, pinch the outer edges up to form a lip. The fruit at the center will remain uncovered by crust.

Bake the *crostata* for approximately 20 minutes until the dough is cooked and the filling bubbly.

Remove and cool slightly before removing it to a serving plate. Cool completely before cutting.

To serve, top each slice with a dollop of whipped cream, lightly sweetened with Splenda if desired.

Drunken Rubies
(Pomegranates in Sweet Red Wine)

SERVES 4

Here's an unusual dessert, very easy to prepare, that makes a smashing impression at dinner. The fact that pomegranates have recently become the antioxidant darlings of the nutritional world is an added bonus to those of us who love to eat them. Although it's gorgeous served in stemmed glasses, it can also be used as a great topping for low-carb ice cream.

Protein per serving:
0.5 gram

Effective carb per serving:
8 grams
(Based on all the sources we could find, pomegranate seeds are said to contain few grams of fiber. Our eyes and mouths tell us that every kernel contains a seed so large that it seems it's half seed. How, therefore, it could be true that a serving could contain only 0.3 gram of fiber for 8.3 grams of carb is a mystery to us. But there it is.)

2 pomegranates
4 packets Splenda
zest of 1 lemon
1 cup dry red wine
1 to 2 teaspoons ThickenThin not/Sugar (see page 9) or
    ½ teaspoon xanthan gum (optional)
fresh mint for garnish

Slice open and remove the seeds from the pomegranates, separating them from the white pith and the rind. Put them into a bowl. Use gloves, since the red pomegranate juice will stain your hands and clothes.

In a saucepan over medium-high heat, mix the Splenda and lemon zest with the red wine and bring to a boil. Simmer and reduce by one-half to concentrate the flavor and slightly thicken the syrup. Add the ThickenThin, if desired, to thicken the syrup more quickly and fully.

Pour the mixture over the pomegranates.

Cover tightly and chill for at least 1 hour prior to serving; several hours is fine.

When ready to serve, divide the pomegranate seeds and sweetened wine evenly among four stemmed dessert or martini glasses. Garnish with a mint sprig.

Raspberry Coulis

SERVES 4 TO 6

Drizzled on the dessert plate to dress up a slice of Coconut-Almond Cake (page 186), pooled under a slice of Flourless Chocolate Cake (page 188), or poured over low-carb ice cream, this simple fruit sauce will add a sweet-tart zip and gorgeous color to any presentation.

Protein per serving:
0.7 gram (for 4),
0.5 gram (for 6)

Effective carb per serving:
4.7 grams (for 4),
3.5 grams (for 6)

1 bag (about 10 ounces) frozen unsweetened raspberries, thawed
4 packets Splenda or stevia
1 lemon, juice and zest

Place all the ingredients into a blender or a food processor and puree until smooth.

Use immediately or store in an airtight container for up to 3 days.

Poached Pears in Sweet Cabernet Reduction Sauce

SERVES 4

Elegant and impressive in its presentation, this beautiful dessert is a treat for the eye as well as the palate. Just a drizzle of the sauce is all you need to turn a simple pear into a special-occasion dessert. While the carb count makes this pleasure one more suitable to the low-carb maintenance lifestyle, it's low enough in carb to enjoy once in a while during correction.

Protein per serving:
1.2 grams

Effective carb per serving:
14.2 grams

4 extra-small pears*
1 cup red wine
1 cup water
12 packets Splenda or stevia
1 cinnamon stick
1 lemon, sliced
½ cup heavy cream (optional)

Peel the pears, leaving the stems intact; for larger pears, use a melon baller to remove the core from the blossom (bottom) end of the pear.

In a medium saucepan, combine the wine, water, and sweetener and bring to a boil. Reduce the heat to medium-low. Add the pears, cinnamon stick, and lemon slices and cover. Cook the pears at a simmer for about 20 minutes or until very tender.

Remove the pears to a bowl, cover them, and refrigerate for several hours—overnight if possible. Remove the cinnamon stick, lemon slices, and any stray seeds that may have gotten into the sauce mixture.

Increase the temperature to medium-high and reduce the sauce to a syrupy consistency. Pour it into a clean container, cover, and refrigerate. Remove the sauce at least an hour before serving and let it come to room temperature. Warm it gently in the microwave for 20 seconds on high.

When ready to serve, whip the cream to form soft peaks. Place a couple of tablespoons of whipped cream into the middle of each serving plate, center a pear in the pool of cream, and drizzle the sauce over it.

*If you cannot find extra-small pears, simply use 2 larger ones and serve half a pear, split lengthwise, per dessert. Place the half pears cut side down in the pool of cream.

French Vanilla Ice Cream Deluxe

SERVES 8

A perennial favorite dessert in its own right or as the perfect topper to a warm piece of All-American Apple Pie (page 208) or Flourless Chocolate Cake (page 188), nothing beats the pure simplicity of good vanilla ice cream. This one is low in carb but filled with the full-on goodness (and calories) of heavy cream and eggs.

Protein per serving:
4.7 grams

Effective carb per serving:
4.3 grams

6 egg yolks
16 packets Splenda or stevia
2 tablespoons ThickenThin not/Sugar* (see page 9)
2 cups half-and-half
1 vanilla bean†
1 cup heavy cream

In a bowl, beat the egg yolks with the sweetener and ThickenThin until they are light yellow and thick.

Heat the half-and-half in a saucepan over medium heat.

Split the vanilla bean and scrape out the seeds and add them to the half-and-half. Toss in the vanilla pod as well and continue to gently heat until steam just begins to rise from the surface. Remove the mixture from the heat. Discard the vanilla pod.

Temper the egg mixture by whisking about ½ cup of the hot half-and-half into it in small amounts at a time.

Pour the egg mixture into the remaining hot half-and-half in the saucepan and cook over medium-low heat, stirring constantly, until the mixture thickens slightly and will coat the back of a spoon. Do not let it boil. (Ideally, it should reach 175 degrees on an instant thermometer.)

Strain the custard into a glass bowl (stir in vanilla extract now if you are using it), stir in the heavy cream, taste for sweetness, and add another packet or two of Splenda if you feel it necessary.

*ThickenThin will improve the consistency and help to prevent ice crystals from forming in the ice cream stored in the freezer. It is not absolutely required.

†You can substitute 2 teaspoons of pure vanilla extract for the vanilla bean, but you won't have the lovely little black specks. Don't add the extract until later in the recipe in order to preserve its flavor.

Quickly chill the mixture by placing the bowl half submerged in a pan of ice water, ideally to a temperature of 40 degrees.

Churn the custard according to your ice cream maker's instructions.

When frozen, serve immediately. Store the leftover ice cream in a tightly sealed freezer container and thaw it gently for 20 seconds in the microwave to facilitate scooping.

Bit O' Sweet Glaze

MAKES ENOUGH TO GLAZE ABOUT 100 COOKIES

Sometimes just a little bit of shine and a little bit of sweet can turn an ordinary cookie, muffin, or cake into something fabulous. By diluting the sugar with alternative sweeteners of several types, you can drop the carb counts tremendously. It's even possible, for those who really don't tolerate sugar, to replace all the sugar by using 1 tablespoon each of the nonsugar sweeteners for a minimal decrease in quality. Remember, though, that you'll be using a tiny amount on each serving; even if you were to use all real sugar the glaze would add only a minuscule 0.3 gram of carb per cookie.

Protein per entire recipe:
5.5 grams

Effective carb per entire recipe:
18.3 grams

2 tablespoons unsifted powdered sugar
1 tablespoon Just Whites (powdered egg whites)
1 tablespoon granular Splenda, erythritol, or xylitol*
⅛ teaspoon pure vanilla, almond, lemon, orange, or coconut extract
2 to 3 teaspoons hot water

In a small bowl, combine the sugar, Just Whites, and sweetener.

Add the extract and hot water and stir until you have a smooth mixture, about the consistency of half-and-half or milk. Add additional water a few drops at a time, if needed, to achieve this thin consistency.

Sparingly spread a thin layer of the glaze onto warm cookies or drizzle it over the top of coffee cake, pound cake, or muffins.

*Xylitol and erythritol are pretty benign sugar alcohols (few gastrointestinal effects, minimal absorption) that are available commercially at many grocery stores, most natural food stores, and online. If you have difficulty finding them, check our Web sites, www.proteinpower.com and lowcarbcookwoRx.com.

Bittersweet Chocolate Glaze

SERVES 12 TO
36, DEPENDING
ON WHAT IS
BEING GLAZED

Great to use on Golden Pound Cake (page 183), on low-carb cook-ies or biscotti, or on your favorite low-carb coffee cakes, this easy and very chocolaty topping provides an intense bit of flavor and sweetness for the carb load. This recipe will glaze a large loaf, a 9-inch single-layer cake, or dozens of cookies or biscotti. It even makes a good crisp-shell topping for low-carb ice cream or large, fresh strawberries.

Protein per recipe:
1.3 grams (for 12),
0.4 grams (for 36)

*Effective carb
per recipe:*
4.4 grams (for 12),
1.5 grams (for 36)

¾ cup premium unsweetened Dutch process cocoa powder
½ cup heavy cream
6 tablespoons unsalted butter, cut into small pieces
¾ cup granular Splenda
pinch salt (or to taste)
½ teaspoon vanilla extract

Mix all the ingredients, except the vanilla, in a small saucepan.
    Cook over low heat, stirring with a heatproof spatula or a wooden spoon until melted, smooth, and thickened, 5 to 7 minutes.
    Remove from the heat and stir in the vanilla extract.
    Use immediately, while still warm.

Classic Chocolate Truffles

**MAKES ABOUT
30 TRUFFLES**

Rich and intensely chocolate, these luscious little bites have all the sensuous flavor of the original with many fewer carbs, yet they are so easy to make that even novice candy makers can turn out delectable delights for friends and family. A dozen of these, in a pretty box with tissue, make as impressive and welcome a gift as flowers or wine . . . to a chocolate lover, maybe even a better one.

Protein each:
1.1 grams

Effective carb each:
3.1 grams

8 ounces unsweetened premium baking chocolate, finely chopped
¾ stick (6 tablespoons) unsalted butter, cut into pieces
1 egg yolk
1 cup granular Splenda
15 packets Splenda
⅓ cup unsweetened Dutch process cocoa powder

Melt the chocolate and butter in a large heatproof mixing bowl placed over a pan of barely simmering water. Stir frequently until completely melted and smooth. Remove from the heat.

Place the eggs and all the Splenda into another heatproof mixing bowl and beat with a whisk; place the bowl over the pan of simmering water and continue to whisk until the yolk mixture thickens to the consistency of heavy cream (ideally, to a temperature of 165 degrees on an instant thermometer).

Fold the yolk mixture into the melted chocolate just until incorporated and smooth.

If you really want the truffles perfectly smooth, press the mixture through a mesh strainer.

Cover the bowl and chill for at least 2 hours until firm.

Remove the truffle mixture from the refrigerator and allow it to soften slightly at room temperature for about 30 minutes.

Place the cocoa powder into a pie plate or a wide shallow bowl.

With a 1-inch melon baller, scoop up balls of the truffle mixture, form into irregular spheres with your hands, and drop them into the cocoa powder. Repeat until you have a plateful.

Shake the pie plate gently to coat the truffles with cocoa powder; shake off the excess, and place the finished truffles onto a sheet of waxed paper. Repeat until all the truffles are formed and dusted.

Cover and refrigerate for several hours. Transfer the truffles to a container and store, tightly covered, in the refrigerator for up to 2 weeks.

If you wish to freeze the truffles, form the truffle mixture into spheres but do not dust them with the cocoa. Simply freeze in a single layer, and when frozen, place into a ziplock freezer bag until ready to use; they'll keep frozen for up to 3 months. When ready to use, thaw in the refrigerator overnight, warm at room temperature for 30 minutes, and finish by coating the truffles with the cocoa powder.

Traditional Shortbread Cookies

**MAKES ABOUT
30 COOKIES**

We love these shortbread cookies just as they are, touched with a little Bit O' Sweet Glaze (page 219), half-dipped in Bittersweet Chocolate Glaze (page 220), or even sprinkled with just a few crystals of large-grained natural sugar if you're in the mood for a bit of a splurge—after all, ⅛ teaspoon of sugar will add only 0.7 gram of carb per cookie. While they don't quite have the crispy snap of the original, they've got the buttery taste.

*Protein per
serving:*
2.3 grams

*Effective carb
per serving:*
3.5 grams
(unglazed and
unsprinkled)

⅜ cup polydextrose powder*
1¼ cups almond flour
¼ cup all-purpose flour
¼ cup cornstarch
⅛ teaspoon salt
1½ sticks (12 tablespoons) unsalted butter, softened to room temperature
12 packets of Splenda or stevia†
1 egg yolk

Combine the polydextrose powder, almond flour, all-purpose flour, cornstarch, and salt in a bowl.

In a separate bowl, using an electric mixer on low speed, mix together the butter and sweetener until just combined.

Still on low speed, beat the egg yolk into the butter mixture. Take over by hand and fold in the dry ingredients, mixing just until the dough comes together and no dry ingredients remain visible.

Turn the dough onto a piece of waxed paper and shape it into a cylindrical or rectangular log. Wrap securely and chill for at least a

*Polydextrose is a slightly sweet, mostly indigestible starch (like fiber) available online. You may substitute an additional ¼ cup of wheat flour plus 1 tablespoon of Thicken-Thin not/Sugar for it in this recipe, for an increase in effective carb of a little over half a gram per cookie.

†If you do not like Splenda or stevia, another option is to use ½ cup of granular xylitol or erythritol. Xylitol and erythritol are pretty benign sugar alcohols (few gastrointestinal effects, minimal absorption) that are available commercially at many grocery stores, most natural food stores, and online. If you have difficulty finding them, check our Web sites, www.proteinpower.com and lowcarbcookwoRx.com. If you use xylitol or erythritol, reduce the polydextrose powder to ¼ cup.

half hour before proceeding. (The wrapped log can be placed into a ziplock freezer bag to keep for future baking up to 6 weeks later. It's best to bake the cookies in small batches to be eaten fresh rather than in large batches to store.)

Preheat the oven to 275 degrees.

Slice the chilled dough into ¼-inch-thick pieces, place about two inches apart on the baking sheet, and bake for about 25 minutes. For a little more sweetness, top each piece with a small bit of sugar; then sprinkle about ⅛ teaspoon of large grained sugar onto the raw sliced cookie and press it in very slightly with your fingers before baking. Do not let the cookies brown; they should be firmly set but still tender.

Cool the cookies on the baking sheet, then remove them gently with a spatula onto a serving plate.

If glazing, add a teaspoon of glaze or chocolate dip after the cookies have cooled.

Handmade Marshmallows

MAKES ABOUT
FORTY 1-INCH
MARSHMALLOWS

The delight of children for ages, the marshmallow is nothing more than a sweet meringue gelatin and is amenable to low-carb adaptation. This recipe will make more than enough to top our Butternut Squash Casserole (page 147), so you'll have plenty to add to low-carb hot chocolate. Be advised, though, that because they lack sugar, these don't hold up to toasting by the fire.

Protein per serving:
0.7 gram

Effective carb per serving:
0.3 gram

3 envelopes unflavored gelatin
¾ cup plus ¼ cup (cold) water (divided for use)
2 teaspoons vanilla extract (or other flavoring of choice)
¼ cup granular Splenda
3 egg whites

Sprinkle the gelatin over ¼ cup of the cold water in a small bowl and allow the gelatin to bloom and soften for about 5 minutes.

Meanwhile, bring the remaining ¾ cup of water to a boil in a small saucepan.

Add the softened gelatin to the boiling water, whisking to mix thoroughly until the gelatin is completely dissolved. Remove from the heat, stir in the vanilla and Splenda, and allow the mixture to cool to the consistency of thick syrup.

When ready to proceed, in a small mixing bowl, use an electric mixer to beat the egg whites to soft peaks. Drizzle a slow, thin stream of the gelatin mixture into the egg whites, beating all the while to fully incorporate the gelatin. Continue to beat to a light, fluffy (not dry) consistency.

Pour the mixture into a shallow pan, cool until set, and cut to your desired size. Be aware that without the light cornstarch coating of commercial marshmallows, the pieces will stick together.* Alternatively, pour the mixture into a clean container with a tight-fitting lid to use by the spoonful as marshmallow cream. The marshmallows will keep for a few days in the refrigerator.

*To prevent sticking, you can toss them in some polydextrose powder (available online) for a negligible increase in carbs per marshmallow.

Guiltless Margaritas

SERVES 4

There's something magical about sipping a good margarita as the Santa Fe sun goes down, and we've sipped our fair share. Unfortunately, most commercially made margarita mixes are mainly high-fructose corn syrup. We prefer ours with real lime juice, sweetened with a low-carb simple syrup made with artificial or carb-free natural sweeteners.

Protein per serving:
0.3 gram

Effective carb per serving:
7.1 grams

1 cup cold water
12 packets stevia or Splenda
zest of 1 orange
1 tablespoon ThickenThin not/Sugar (see page 9) or
    2 teaspoons xanthan gum
1 cup fresh lime juice
1½ cups tequila
4 lime slices (for garnish)

In a small saucepan, combine the water with the sweetener and the orange zest. Sprinkle in the ThickenThin and stir to dissolve, breaking up any lumps that form.

Heat gently to thicken slightly, then remove from the heat to cool.
In a 2-quart pitcher, mix the lime juice, cooled syrup, and tequila.
Chill, if possible, for at least an hour.
Moisten the rim of four wide-mouthed glasses with lime juice or water and invert into coarse salt, if desired.
Pour the chilled margaritas into the glasses over crushed ice.
Garnish with the lime slices.

Guiltless Mojitos

SERVES 4

The Mojito, always a popular libation in South America and the tropics, gained increased fame when it was featured on the beach in a recent 007 flick. This is clearly another drink that cries out to be shaken, not stirred!

Protein per serving:
0.3 gram

Effective carb per serving:
7.1 grams

1½ cups cold water
15 packets stevia or Splenda
1 tablespoon ThickenThin not/Sugar (see page 9) or
    2 teaspoons xanthan gum
2 cups mint leaves and stems
½ cup fresh lime juice
1 cup light rum
4 lime slices (for garnish)

In a small saucepan, combine the water with the sweetener. Sprinkle in the ThickenThin and whisk to dissolve, breaking up any lumps that form. Add 2 or 3 mint sprigs.

Heat gently to thicken slightly, then remove from the heat to cool. Infuse the mint into the syrup. When completely cool, remove the mint sprigs.

In a 2-quart pitcher, mix the lime juice, cooled syrup, and rum.

Chill, if possible, for at least an hour.

Divide the remaining fresh mint among four tall chilled glasses; crush it with a spoon to slightly bruise it.

Fill the glasses with crushed ice and pour the chilled Mojitos over or, if you prefer, shake the glasses with crushed ice to chill even further and strain the Mojitos into each mint-filled glass.

Garnish with the lime slices.

Traditional Eggnog

SERVES 10

At our house, Christmas just isn't Christmas without a big punch bowl of creamy, rich homemade eggnog. We whip up a batch on Christmas Eve, another on Christmas Day, and usually one more on New Year's Day. Whatever the holiday traditions at your house, if you love real eggnog, you'll treasure this recipe as we do.

Protein per serving:
9 grams

Effective carb per serving:
7.1 grams

2 cups half-and-half
2 cups water
1 cup granular Splenda* (divided for use)
1 tablespoon pure vanilla extract
12 large eggs, separated (refrigerate egg whites in a covered container)
2 cups heavy cream
1 cup brandy, chilled
1 cup bourbon, chilled
¼ teaspoon freshly grated nutmeg (for garnish)

In a saucepan over medium heat, combine the half-and-half, water, ½ of the Splenda, and the vanilla and bring just to a boil. Remove from the heat.

In a bowl, beat the egg yolks for 2 or 3 minutes until they turn a pale yellow and thicken. Slowly pour in about ½ cup of the hot half-and-half, whisking constantly, to temper the eggs. Pour the tempered egg mixture into the saucepan and whisk to combine.

Cook over medium heat, stirring constantly, for about 5 minutes until the mixture coats the back of a spoon. Remove from the heat and strain through a mesh strainer into a clean bowl or a pitcher. Cover the surface with plastic to prevent a skin from forming. Chill for several hours or overnight.

*You can reduce the carb content a bit further by using 24 packets of Splenda or stevia in place of the cup of granular Splenda for very little loss of volume or texture. The packets, with less bulking agent, count as 1 gram per packet; the granular has been counted at 48 grams per cup, but remember that there is debate over the degree to which the maltodextrin isomer used in granular Splenda is absorbable.

When ready to proceed, beat the egg whites with an electric mixer to form soft peaks. Continue beating as you gradually add ¼ cup of Splenda. Beat the whites until stiff peaks form.

In a separate bowl, beat the heavy cream for a minute or two, add the remaining ¼ cup of Splenda, and continue beating until soft peaks form.

Pour the chilled egg yolk mixture into a large punch bowl and add the alcohol, stirring to mix. Fold in the whipped cream and the egg whites, garnish with a sprinkle of nutmeg, and enjoy.

Parisian-Style Hot Cho-Co-Late

MAKES ABOUT
4 CUPS,
8 SERVINGS

On trips to Paris, we always indulge in an afternoon stop at Angelina, the famous tea salon on the rue de Rivoli, across from the Tuileries. Their signature hot chocolate, thick and silky, comes served in a warm silver pot with a dish of sweetened whipped cream on the side. This recipe, made with coconut milk, rivals the original in taste in texture, with all the healthful qualities of cocoa and coconut. Sip it slowly and savor the pure joy.

Protein per serving:
3.6 grams

Effective carb per serving:
7 grams

1 can (14 ounces) premium unsweetened coconut milk
2 cups water
6 tablespoons granular Splenda
6 packets Splenda
¼ cup unsweetened Dutch process cocoa powder
6 ounces unsweetened premium baking chocolate, finely chopped
1 teaspoon pure vanilla extract

GARNISH
¼ cup heavy cream
2 packets Splenda

In a medium-size heavy saucepan, whisk together the coconut milk, water, all the Splenda, and the cocoa powder. Warm the mixture over medium heat, stirring to dissolve the cocoa.

Add the chopped chocolate and stir until it melts completely.

Increase the heat to medium-high to bring the mixture to a simmer but do not boil.

Reduce the heat to medium and cook for 5 minutes, stirring occasionally.

Meanwhile, for the garnish, whip the cream until frothy, add the 2 packets of Splenda, and continue to whip until soft peaks form.

Remove the hot chocolate from the heat and stir in the vanilla extract.

Place a dollop of whipped cream on top of each serving.

VARIATION

All-Dairy Traditional Cocoa. Substitute 2 cups of milk and 2 cups of half-and-half for the coconut milk and water for an even creamier all-dairy alternative. Be aware that the carb count will rise only minimally, but the calorie count will go up a fair amount.

CHAPTER 9

◇   ◇   ◇

Kid Stuff

Hi-Pro French Toast Fingers

Stealthy Garden Pizza

Kidpasta Bowties

Stealthy Healthy Pasta Sauce

Double Red Soup

Invisible Vegetable Hamburger Soup

Hobo Healthburgers

Chicken Zoo Bites

Simple Cheese Quesadilla

Frozen Fruit Skewers

Cocopro Pudding

◇   ◇   ◇

◇　◇　◇

In the collective unconscious of most parents resides a vision. In it, their smiling children come to the table, fold their freshly washed hands, and happily gobble up whatever nutritious food lies before them on their plates. Some parents draw a lucky hand in that regard, with kids who will eat pretty much anything that's put in front of them. Other kids are far more finicky about what they will and won't eat and, with noses wrinkled in utter disgust, will diligently pick out every microscopic speck that even looks like it might at one time have been, for instance, broccoli, an onion, or a bell pepper. We had one of each and one that fell sort of in between.

Our youngest son was a card-carrying member of the diligent picker club; he could spot a fleck of tomato or green pea (or just about anything else) at forty paces. For him it was always more the texture of things than their specific taste. He would eat a raw carrot, for instance, but couldn't be force-fed a cooked one. Consequently, we brought him up never to impolitely declare that he didn't like something offered to him but rather, if asked, to simply state that he hadn't yet acquired the taste for fill-in-the-blank. That was back when we entertained the hope that someday he *would* acquire the taste for something besides meat, any style, pepperoni or hamburger pizza, and crescent rolls. Even as an adult—to our everlasting dismay—there are still precious few foods he actually likes, albeit it's a broader palate than it once was, and he will, as Mom would have said, take a bite to be polite.

Many of our Kid Stuff recipes were born of necessity from the fertile ground of cooking for a child who loved meat loaf as long as he couldn't see the vegetables in it. This was a child who would eat every bite of beef in the stew, practically lick the thick broth from the bowl, and leave an untouched mound of vegetables in the bottom. We determined long ago that we'd get the veggies into him by hook or by crook, and a whole array of stealth recipes resulted. Many of them take a little help from the grocery store, using baby-food vegetables, already smoothly pureed and wholesome, to add nutrition in unexpected places, such as our Stealthy Healthy Pasta Sauce and Hobo Healthburgers.

The same technique, sort of in reverse, can be used to get protein into picky adolescents and preteenagers—most often girls—who suddenly declare themselves vegetarian for no apparent reason, by which they usually don't mean to imply a desire to consume more vegetables, but rather to declare their intention of subsisting on a diet of cheese pizza, bagels, French fries, diet soda, and Twinkies. (We're not suggesting here that you should necessarily undermine a well-thought-out vegetarian ideology; rather we suggest that you may wish to use these techniques to negotiate your way around a case of temporary peer-pressure-driven vegetarian dabbling without making a federal case of it.) It's easy to puree chicken breast, turkey breast, or deli ham slices to a smooth consistency with a little chicken broth and fold that good protein right into the pizza or pasta sauce.

No matter what the genesis of the adolescent pickiness, with these recipes the family table doesn't have to become a nightly battleground. They're based on the foods kids love to eat, yet prepared with a stealthy twist that will keep them happily eating nutritious food without even knowing it. Just to give them a little practice at it, we'd also advise introducing the typical grown-up versions of foods to kids regularly—put a small pile of green peas, beets, or a broccoli floret or two on the plate beside the Chicken Zoo Bites or Stealthy Garden Pizza; use the take-a-bite-to-be-polite philosophy. Even if they don't eat much of it, you can rest assured that they've still been well fed. Until they're much older, they'll never need to know about the veggies in the sauce.

Hi-Pro French Toast Fingers

SERVES 4

Who doesn't love French toast for breakfast? Here's a quick and easy lower-carb version with an added punch of extra protein to get kids and adults off to a good start. Trim the bread and make the egg mixture the night before, and you'll have them on the griddle in no time.

Protein per serving:
17.2 grams

Effective carb per serving:
12.3 grams
(Does not include syrup or other topping.)

8 slices commercial low-carb bread
3 eggs
¾ cup half-and-half
1 scoop (about 20 grams) vanilla or natural flavor
    low-carb whey protein powder
½ teaspoon vanilla
2 packets Splenda
pinch nutmeg (or to taste)
1 to 2 tablespoons unsalted butter

Trim the crust from the bread; cut the bread into fingers by cutting in half or thirds lengthwise.* (If not cooking right away, store them overnight in a ziplock bag.)

In a shallow bowl, beat the eggs until light yellow. Whisk in the half-and-half, protein powder, vanilla, Splenda, and nutmeg. (If not cooking right away, store the egg mixture in a container with a tight-fitting lid, refrigerated, overnight. Thin with a little water if it thickens overnight.)

Melt butter on a griddle or a skillet over medium heat.

Dip each finger into the egg batter and fry the fingers until golden brown; turn and brown evenly on other side.

Remove to a warm plate to hold until the entire batch has been cooked.

Top with melted butter and Almost Real Maple Syrup (page 26), commercial low-carb syrup, or Maple Surple (page 27).

*Make bread crumbs of the saved crusts by pulsing them in a food processor. Store them in ziplock freezer bags until you're ready to use them.

Stealthy Garden Pizza

MAKES 4
INDIVIDUAL
PIZZAS

There's nothing kids love better than pizza, and if you play it right, it can be a very healthy meal. Even if your kids turn up their noses at any colorful thing resembling a vegetable—as our youngest son did—they'll never spot one here. With this dish, they'll eat their veggies and ask for more. Just one will fill even the hollow leg of an adolescent boy; younger kids or those with smaller appetites can happily split a pizza.

Protein per pizza:
37.6 grams
(The protein and
carb counts for this
recipe are for a
whole pizza, a por-
tion suitable for
teens and adults.
For smaller chil-
dren, half or one-
third of a pizza
should be enough.)

*Effective carb
per pizza:*
17.2 grams

4 Cheesy Waffle Pizza Platforms (page 68)
1 can (14 ounces) plain pizza sauce
1 jar (4 ounces) baby-food peas or green beans
1 jar (4 ounces) baby-food carrots or winter squash
4 ounces sliced provolone cheese
2 cups shredded mozzarella cheese

Preheat the oven to 400 degrees.

Place the waffles onto a cookie or baking sheet and crisp them slightly in the oven for a minute or two, then remove them.

In a bowl, combine the pizza sauce and baby-food veggies until thoroughly blended.

Cover each waffle with a layer of provolone slices.

Ladle about ⅓ cup of the pizza sauce onto each waffle and spread evenly almost to the edges.

Top each pizza with ½ cup of the shredded mozzarella.

Bake in the oven for 5 to 7 minutes until the cheese is completely melted. Serve immediately.

VARIATION

Meat Lovers' Garden Pizza. If your pizza fans love meat on their pizza, by all means add a couple of ounces of pepperoni, cooked ham-burger, or cooked sausage before adding the mozzarella cheese. Each ounce of meat will add 6 or 7 grams of protein to the total.

Kidpasta Bowties

SERVES 4

Kids will love the shape of these little bites of pasta because the cheesy sauce will stick to them well. You won't even need a pasta machine, because they're very easy to make by hand. Make a double batch, cook some fresh, and freeze the rest to use later.

Protein per serving:
25.4 grams

Effective carb per serving:
5.0 grams
(For the pasta only, no sauce.)

½ recipe Impasta (page 143)

Roll the dough into a sheet no thicker than ⅛ inch. Cut with a crimping tool or a pizza cutter to make long strips about 1-inch wide, then cut again across the strips at 2-inch intervals to make rectangles.

Pinch each rectangle in the center between your thumb and forefinger to make the bowtie.

Drop fresh into boiling salted water and cook for 4 to 6 minutes until al dente.

Drain very well and toss with Stealthy Healthy Pasta Sauce (page 238).

To save the bowties, dry them overnight on the countertop, covered with a clean kitchen towel, then freeze them in a single layer on a baking sheet for several hours or overnight. Store ½- to 1-cup portions in ziplock bags for up to 6 weeks. Allow the pasta to thaw before cooking.

Stealthy Healthy Pasta Sauce

SERVES 8

Sure, kids love pasta, as long as it's simple and cheesy. You, as a parent, would like it to provide them with good-quality protein, good-quality fats, and plenty of veggies. Dream on, you say? This recipe will please you both, as it's filled with all the good things growing kids need and not a speck of a vegetable visible for them to pick out.

Protein per serving:
6.6 grams (sauce only),
32 grams (with pasta)

Effective carb per serving:
4.1 grams (sauce only),
9.1 (with pasta)

4 ounces deli-sliced cooked chicken, coarsely diced
2 tablespoons olive oil
2 tablespoons chicken broth (or as needed)
1 can (about 14 ounces) tomato sauce
1 jar (4 ounces) baby-food peas or green beans
1 jar (4 ounces) baby-food carrots or winter squash
½ teaspoon salt
½ teaspoon finely ground dried basil
½ teaspoon finely ground dried oregano
¼ teaspoon garlic powder
¼ teaspoon finely ground black pepper
4 tablespoons grated Parmesan cheese (optional)
1 recipe cooked Kidpasta Bowties (page 237)*

Place the chicken and olive oil into a food processor; pulse a few times, then puree till smooth, adding a tablespoon or two of chicken broth if needed to make the process easier.

Add all the remaining ingredients and process until completely smooth and uniform in color. At this point, you may put the sauce into a clean container with a tight-fitting lid and store it in the refrigerator for several days.

When ready to serve, warm the sauce gently over a medium flame. If making the full recipe, pour the sauce over 4 cups of cooked,

*You may substitute commercial low-carb pasta or any sort of whole-grain pasta you wish your child to eat; the former won't be as tasty and the latter won't be as high in protein or as carb friendly, but they're less fuss.

drained Kidpasta Bowties or low-carb or whole-wheat pasta and toss to coat. (If making a single serving, pour ¼ of the sauce over a cup of cooked pasta.)

Top each serving with a sprinkling of grated parmesan, if desired.

VARIATION

Baked Bowties. After topping the pasta with the sauce, turn the pasta into an oiled baking dish, sprinkle on ½ cup of grated mozzarella cheese, and bake in a 350-degree oven until the cheese is melted and bubbly. (Approximately 1 tablespoon of cheese per serving will add 1.4 grams of protein and negligible carb grams to each portion.)

Double Red Soup

SERVES 4

It looks like simple tomato soup but has the added nutritional kick of roasted red peppers and the fabulous antioxidants they contain. Serve it hot with a grilled cheese sandwich, and we think you'll please the most finicky eaters. Even adults will enjoy it, topped with a dollop of sour cream and a sprinkling of fresh herbs. The recipe multiplies well for bigger crowds.

Protein per serving:
2.8 grams

Effective carb per serving:
8.9 grams

1 jar (12 ounces) roasted red peppers
1 can (about 15 ounces) diced tomatoes
2 cups vegetable broth
½ teaspoon salt
¼ teaspoon finely ground black pepper

Drain and remove the seeds from the red peppers.

Place all the ingredients into a blender or a food processor and blend until smooth. If you have a really picky youngster and wish to achieve a perfectly smooth result, press the mixture through a screen strainer. At this point, you can refrigerate the soup in a sealed container for several days.

Heat the soup thoroughly and serve.

Invisible Vegetable Hamburger Soup

SERVES 4

When our youngest son was small, he loved the beef and the broth of soup but would diligently pick out even the smallest speck of anything that resembled a vegetable, leaving it in the bottom of the bowl. Although he's all grown up now, he still has eyes like an eagle and can spot a fleck of parsley at thirty paces. In our ongoing quest to feed him well, we had to get creative. If you've got a picky eater at home, this invisible vegetable version should help keep the peace at the dinner table.

Protein per serving:
13.8 grams

Effective carb per serving:
6.8 grams

1 tablespoon olive oil
½ sweet onion, chopped
1 clove garlic, chopped
1 jar (4 ounces) baby-food green beans
1 jar (4 ounces) baby-food carrots
1 can (15 ounces) diced tomatoes
½ pound ground sirloin (or very lean ground beef)
1 teaspoon salt
½ teaspoon white pepper
1 quart beef broth

Place the olive oil into a skillet over medium heat and sauté the onion and garlic until limp.

Put the cooked onion and garlic into a food processor or a blender, add the baby food and the tomatoes and their juice, and puree until quite smooth.

In a soup pot over medium heat, place the ground beef, salt, and pepper and cook until no pink remains in the meat. Discard any fat that accumulates.

VARIATION
Instead of beef, use ground turkey or pork and chicken broth for a different taste.

Add the pureed vegetables and the beef broth and bring to a boil; reduce the heat to a simmer and cook for about 10 more minutes.

Serve hot or to save for future use, allow the soup to cool, cover it, and refrigerate for up to several days. (To save time if packing soup for lunches, pour individual servings into plastic containers with tightly fitting lids and refrigerate.) Reheat the pot of soup on the stove top or individual servings in the microwave.

Hobo Healthburgers

SERVES 4

Kids love hobo meals, whether cooked in the oven or over a camp-fire. More like a veggie meat loaf, these hamburgers are filled with stealth nutrients that your kids will never see. We think they'll declare them, as our boys did, the best hamburgers they ever ate. The healthy secret will be yours to keep.

Protein per serving:
27.6 grams

Effective carb per serving:
3.6 grams

1 pound ground sirloin (or very lean ground beef)
1 jar (4 ounces) baby-food green beans or peas
1 jar (4 ounces) baby-food winter squash or carrots
1 tablespoon soy sauce
½ teaspoon garlic powder
½ teaspoon onion powder
½ teaspoon white pepper
4 slices American or mild cheddar cheese (optional)

In a large bowl, combine all the ingredients and work by hand or with a wooden spoon until the vegetables are completely incorporated and invisible.

Form into 4 thick burgers.

Place each burger onto a square (about 12 inches) of aluminum foil. If you'd like, top each patty with a slice of cheese. (The cheese will melt and form a cheesy sauce.)

Bring the four corners to the center and crimp the seams to make a sealed packet.

Place onto a baking tray (or onto the grate over a campfire) and bake at medium-high heat (about 350 degrees) for 30 minutes or until done.

Open the packets and serve.

Chicken Zoo Bites

SERVES 4

Sometimes all it takes to get kids to eat something is to make it into interesting shapes; animal shapes seem to be a hit with most kids, so we decided to make a zoo. Let your child help decide what zoo animals he or she wants for dinner. The inspiration for this recipe came from a creative mother of three boys who tempted them to eat their chicken by making chicken stars with her trusty cookie cutter.

Protein per serving:
26 grams
(This calculation is based on the protein content of the full-size fillet, about 3 to 4 ounces. Depending on the efficiency with which you cut the shapes and the amount of scraps left over, the actual protein per serving will be less.)

Effective carb per serving:
0 grams

4 thin, boneless, skinless chicken breast fillets (about ¼ inch thick)*
1 teaspoon salt
½ teaspoon white pepper
2 tablespoons unsalted butter

Using sharp metal cookie cutters and working on a cutting board, use firm pressure to cut the desired shapes from each fillet, just as though you were cutting out sugar cookies. Try to get two or three animals per fillet and use up most of the chicken. Freeze any leftover edges for later use—to put into a pot of soup or to poach for chicken salad.

Season both sides of each zoo bite with a little bit of salt and pepper.

Melt the butter in a skillet and when foamy, place the zoo bites into the pan and let them cook, undisturbed, for a couple of minutes until golden on the first side. Flip and cook the other side a couple of minutes.

Serve warm.

VARIATION

Zoo Bites in Pasta Sauce. If your child loves tomato sauce—and many do—before removing the zoo bites from the skillet, pour on some Stealthy Healthy Pasta Sauce (page 238) and warm it through as the chicken finishes cooking for a full-court press of veggies they'll never see coming. The sauce adds 3.5 grams of effective carb per ½-cup serving.

*You can usually find thinly sliced breast fillets at your grocer's meat counter, but if you cannot, simply pound a boneless skinless breast until thin.

Simple Cheese Quesadilla

SERVES 1

Kids love melted cheese on almost anything, so there's nothing fancy here, just the taste they love. This very plain quesadilla is sure to win fans at your house. It's so quick and easy to make that bigger kids can learn to make their own, and that's a great way to get them interested in cooking and in nutrition. For a nutritious meal, pair with a mug of Double Red Soup (page 240).

Protein per serving:
31 grams

Effective carb per serving:
10.6 grams

1 large (burrito size) low-carb flour tortilla*
½ cup shredded Mexican four-cheese blend
¼ cup shredded mozzarella cheese

Heat a griddle or a large skillet and warm the tortilla briefly on one side.

Flip it over and scatter the cheeses over half of the circle.

When the cheeses have melted, fold the empty half of the tortilla over the filling and press slightly to seal it.

Transfer to a cutting board and slice the half-moon into wedges for serving.

*For smaller kids, use the taco-size smaller tortillas to make the wedges a friendlier size for little hands.

Frozen Fruit Skewers

MAKES 12
SKEWERS

Most kids love to eat frozen treats such as ice cream or Popsicles. You can use their affection for cold, sweet foods to entice them to make fruit a snack or dessert choice. Almost any fruit will work, but some hold up better than others in the freezer.

Protein per serving:
0.5 gram

Effective carb per serving:
6.6 grams

24 large green seedless grapes
24 medium fresh strawberries, stemmed
12 large blackberries
24 large red or black seedless grapes
3 kiwis, peeled and each cut into 4 cubes

Wash, drain, and prepare all fruit.

Working with bamboo skewers, skewer the fruit as follows: green grape, strawberry with tip down, green grape, blackberry, red grape, kiwi, red grape, strawberry with tip up. Push the fruit closely together to stabilize it.

Wrap each skewer in plastic or press-wrap, place all of them onto a baking tray, and freeze for at least several hours. Store in a ziplock freezer bag.

Cocopro Pudding

SERVES 8

Almost all kids love pudding as a treat; this one also happens to be quite nutritious, so it makes a great after-school snack. Finally, a dessert that kids and parents can agree on! You can make any flavor pudding you like by varying the flavor of the protein powder and replacing the vanilla extract with extracts of other flavors.

Protein per serving:
8 grams

Effective carb per serving:
5.1 grams

3 eggs

1 can (14 ounces) premium unsweetened coconut milk

1 cup half-and-half

1 cup milk

2 scoops (about 40 grams) low-carb whey protein, vanilla flavor

1 tablespoon ThickenThin not/Sugar (see page 9) or
   1 tablespoon cornstarch

4 packets stevia*

⅛ teaspoon fine salt

1 tablespoon unsalted butter

1 teaspoon vanilla extract

In a saucepan, beat the eggs and then add the coconut milk, half-and-half, and milk; whisk to combine. Add the whey protein, ThickenThin, salt, and stevia and whisk vigorously to break up all the lumps.

Cook over medium heat, stirring constantly, until the pudding thickens. Stir in the butter and vanilla.

Serve warm or cool quickly in a bowl half submerged in a pan of ice water. Cover the bowl and refrigerate.

To make single-serving pudding cups, divide the pudding into individual half-cup serving containers with tight-fitting lids and store in the refrigerator for up to 3 days.

*If you do not wish your child to use this naturally sweet herb, you may substitute 2½ tablespoons honey or 3½ tablespoons of dextrose or glucose powder. These will add roughly 5 grams of carb per serving. Sources for the latter are available online. *A note of caution*: children under 3 should not eat raw honey for health reasons.

Index

butter
  garlic herb, 175
  sesame fire, 174
butternut squash
  casserole, 147
  roasted, soup, 86–87

cake. *See also* coffee cake
  coconut-almond, 186–187
  darned good carrot, 190–191
  flourless chocolate, 188–189
  golden pound, 183
  luscious yellow layer, 184–185
calcium, 50, 53
cappuccino, low-carb version of frozen, 52
carrot cake, darned good, 190–191
casserole
  butternut squash, 147
  green pea and asparagus, 149
  seafood, 132–133
cauliflower
  sautéed, with garlic herb butter, 158
  smashed just like potatoes, 153–154
celery root
  diced in clam chowder, 80–81
  fauxtatoes au gratin, 151
  fauxtato salad, 90
  hash brown fauxtatoes, 48
  preparation of, 78
  puree (creamed fauxtatoes), 150
  with rosemary and garlic, oven-roasted, 152
cereal (proatmeal), 24–25
cheese
  blue cheese dressing, 95
  blue cheese Lorraine miniatures, 65
  cheesy waffle pizza platforms, 68
  fauxtatoes au gratin, 151
  feta and olive frittata, 42
  lemon-ricotta flapjacks, 23
  onions au gratin, 159
  Parmesan crisps, 67
  quesadilla, simple, 244
  stealthy garden pizza, 236

cheese quesadilla, simple, 244
chicken
  barbecued hot wings, 116–117
  enchiladas, green chile, 120–121
  garlic herb butter for, 175
  mushroom packets, 125–126
  oven-barbecued hot wings, 118–119
  pan gravy, 166
  potpie, 122–123
  satay, 124
  sesame fire butter for, 174
  spicy southern fried, 114–115
  tapenade for, 165
  Thai peanut sauce, as marinade for, 176
  Thai red chile, 127
  zoo bites, 243
chile
  green, chicken enchiladas, 120–121
  red, rolled enchiladas, 109–110
  Thai red, chicken, 127
chili
  three-alarm, 111–112
  white, 113
chips
  Parmesan crisps, 67
  spicy tortilla triangles, 66
chocolate
  buttercream frosting, 194
  cake, flourless, 188–189
  chewy fudge brownies, 204
  cho-co-late, Parisian-style hot, 230
  glaze, bittersweet, 220
  ice cream browniewiches, 205
  mousse, decadent espresso, 200–201
  truffles, classic, 221–222
cholesterol, 31–32
  oxidized, 32
cinnamon
  pecan-, coffee cake, 19–20
  -piñon power muffins, 17–18
clam chowder, New England–style, 80–81
cocomocha breakfast tonic, 52
coconut
  -almond cake, 186–187

Check the Drs. Eades's Web site for their PBS cooking show at www.lowcarbcookworx.com for

- ◇ Recommended reading

- ◇ Recipes

- ◇ Cooking tips

- ◇ Essays on nutrition, cooking, and eating

- ◇ Links to food purveyors

- ◇ Specialty item sources

- ◇ VHS and DVD copies of *CookwoRx* episodes

- ◇ Nutritional resources

Check the Drs. Eades's official Web site at www.proteinpower.com for

- ◇ Health and nutrition commentary from the Drs. Eades

- ◇ Links to medical and scientific resources

- ◇ Quality nutritional supplements

- ◇ Dieting support groups and discussion board

- ◇ Recommended reading

- ◇ Interactive body-fat analysis

- ◇ Low-carb research bibliographies

- ◇ Information on the ThickenThin products and other items used in the recipes